SHROPSHIRE POSTCARDS FROM THE PAST

LUDLOW AND SOUTH-WEST SHROPSHIRE

SHROPSHIRE POSTCARDS FROM THE PAST
LUDLOW AND SOUTH-WEST SHROPSHIRE

RAY FARLOW AND DAVID TRUMPER

breedon **books**
PUBLISHING

First published in Great Britain in 2005 by
The Breedon Books Publishing Company Limited
Breedon House, 3 The Parker Centre,
Derby, DE21 4SZ.

ISBN 1 85983 488 4

Printed and bound by Cromwell Press, Trowbridge, Wiltshire.

Contents

Acknowledgements

I gratefully acknowledge all the help I have received on my visits to the Shropshire Records and Research Centre. The staff are always cheerful and friendly and keen to help with all my enquiries. I would also like to thank Miss D.M. Evans for sharing her knowledge of Bucknell with me and for adding extra detail to a number of views. Finally I would like to acknowledge the help I have received from articles written in the *Shropshire Star* by Toby Neal and the informative replies by *Star* readers. Both have done a great deal in recent years to reveal our county's interesting past.

Introduction

Shropshire is a large inland county of great diversity, which has been influenced by countless generations from the Celts, Romans, Saxons and Normans through to the present day. Towards the end of the 19th century and into the 20th century many enterprising national and local photographers travelled around the county taking thousands of photographs of people, places and events that were then turned into postcards. Thankfully many of these cards still survive, tucked away in old albums or stored in attics and at the back of drawers and cupboards. They give us an interesting glimpse of how life was at this time and how quickly things have altered during the last century as progress has accelerated. There are thousands of postcard collectors around the country and Shropshire is extremely fortunate to have Ray Farlow, who has accumulated thousands of views of the county, a most valuable archive for local historians, which he so generously shares with others.

The area covered in this volume is south of Shrewsbury and roughly west of a line from the county town down through Ludlow. It is a land containing a huge variety of scenery – rich fertile valleys, open barren moors and heathland, undulating foothills to the heights of the Long Mynd and the boulder-strewn Stiperstones. Within this section there is the beautiful town of Ludlow, which was once described as 'the finest small town in the whole of England'. There are also the smaller market towns of Bishop's Castle, Clun, Craven Arms and Church Stretton, which has also been called 'Little Switzerland' because of its high altitude, hills and wintry scenes. Hundreds of settlements can be found nestling in quiet secluded valleys, on the side of the Long Mynd or around the Stiperstones. They range from the larger villages such as Pontesbury, Minsterley, Dorrington and Bucknell to the smaller hamlets of Newcastle-on-Clun, the Bog and Lydbury North.

Due to its close proximity to Wales, the area has many ancient fortifications such as Clun and Hopton castles and the fortified manor house at Stokesay. As peace emerged along the Welsh Marches, grand houses and estates such as Plowden Hall and Whitton Court were developed, while in the 18th and 19th century rich industrialists erected such fine buildings as Downton Castle and Stokesay Court.

It is an area of which the poet A.E. Housman wrote:

> *In Valley of Springs and Rivers,*
> *By Onney, Teme and Clun,*
> *The country for easy livers,*
> *The quietest under the sun.*

Chapter One
Market Towns

The photographer is standing in the Bull Ring in Ludlow, looking towards King Street, which is also known as the Narrows. The policeman is standing outside Wainwright's shop. The business was established in 1879 as a boot and shoemakers before becoming a saddlers and expanding into other types of leather goods. By 1960 it was known as the Bull Ring Gift Shop and sold a variety of fancy goods. Although the shop has closed, the area is still known as Wainwright's Corner. W.H. Smith first appeared in Ludlow in around 1880, when they opened a kiosk at the town's railway station before moving into this shop in about 1903. Four years later in May 1907 the citizens of Ludlow were invited to inspect the bookshop when it reopened after extensive improvements. The timber-framed building on the left is the Bull Ring Tavern and the building next door with the Royal Warrant is a chemist's shop founded by George Woodhouse.

In the 1880s the timber-framed building in the centre belonged to Dawes & Bowen, who were wine and spirit importers, while in the building to the left they sold beer and ale. By 1900 the buildings were known as the Vaults and were owned by Allsopp's Brewery of Burton-on-Trent. The premises consisted of three bars, a smoke room, a market room and accommodation for travellers in seven bedrooms. The inn was renamed Ye Olde Bull Ring Tavern in 1931. The building to the right was also an inn called the Bear that was in existence from about 1635 until 1810, when it was converted into a chemist's shop. In 1896 the business was listed as an 'agricultural, family & dispensing chemist and druggist and seedsman, registered dentist & co.; depot for photographers' materials and chemicals; deputy registrar of births and deaths & vaccination officer for Ludlow sub-district'. The Royal Warrant dates from 1909 when the Princess of Wales, who later became Queen Mary, patronised the shop and according to local tradition purchased a toothbrush. The shop was taken over by Boots in the 1930s.

This view of the main A49 leading down to Ludford Bridge and Lower Broad Street was taken around 1930. On the left is the Charlton Arms sporting two Automobile Association badges and advertising luncheons, teas with Hovis and accommodation. The bridge dates from mediaeval times and until the new bypass was built in 1977 was the cause of a number of traffic problems. The man on the right with the white hat and armbands appears to be an AA or RAC patrol officer. On the other side of the bridge is the petrol pump of Temeside Garage, which was housed on the site of the 13th-century Hospital of St John the Baptist. A fragment of the old building can be seen facing the bridge. The timber-framed house just above is the Bell Inn that was in operation from about 1822 until 1896.

Lower Broad Street is the area where the people involved in Ludlow's cloth industry lived. The building on the left was once known as Teme Mill and was built in the 19th century by William Evans, a cloth manufacturer. For many years Bodenham and Sons Ltd, who ran several businesses in the town, used it as a warehouse. At the top of the bank is the Broad Gate, the last of the five main gateways into Ludlow. The white building to the right of the gate is the Wheatsheaf, the last of nine public houses that once existed in this part of the town. The timber-framed building on the right once housed an inn called the Bell, which occupies part of the site of the Hospital of St John the Baptist dating back to the 13th century. Towards the end of the 19th century magistrates refused to renew its licence after a number of incidents of unruly behaviour.

The police officer on the left seems to have his eye on the innocent-looking young boy in this fine view of the Bull Ring in the late 1950s. Note the cars parked outside the beautiful timber-framed buildings of Boots' chemist shop and the Bull Ring Tavern, who were selling Ind Coope, Allsopp and Double Diamond beer at this time. Another chemist called Brown and Francis occupies the building on the right. William Brown was first listed there in around 1905 when he was also manager of the Shropshire Horse and Cattle Food Company. The building on the left is the rear of the Tolsey, which was built in the 15th century. The 'Court of Pye Powder' was held there to settle disputes in the market place quickly, before the dust was shaken from their feet. The building was occupied in the 1950s by Handy's, who were florists, greengrocers and fruiterers.

The timber-framed building with the 'GRILL' sign on the first storey is the Angel Hotel. It is first mentioned as a hostelry in 1551 and it maintained the same name throughout its history. In 1900 the hotel was owned by W.E. Sharp of Castle House, Ludlow, and its accommodation consisted of a bar, two parlours, a commercial and coffee room, a billiard room and 18 bedrooms with stabling at the rear for 18 horses. De Greys Café sign can be seen on the next timber-framed house, hanging just above an RAC sign. The building once housed an inn called the Swann until it was taken over by Herbert Smith, a fashionable boot and shoemaker. De Greys opened there in the 1920s and was advertised as one of the larger and finer café-restaurants in the Midlands. They were also listed as confectioners, pastry cooks and chocolate manufacturers.

This is a view of the Bull Ring, looking down towards Corve Street in the 1950s. The elaborately carved timber-framed house on the right is the famous Feathers Hotel. It was the home of Rees Jones, a lawyer at the Council of the Marches, and his initials can still be seen on the lock plate of the main door. It became an inn around 1670 and by 1900 it was listed as a 'First Class Family and Commercial Hotel and Posting House'. By the 1960s it was advertised as having 25 cosy bedrooms with hot and cold water and slot fires and, as one of the most famous hotels in the country, they were visited 'by sightseers and lovers of old-world England, from all parts of the world'. On the opposite side of the road is the sign of the Bull Hotel, a 15th-century inn with a Georgian-style frontage after a fire destroyed the old façade in 1794.

This is a view across the Castle Square to the Town Hall, which was built in 1887 to commemorate the Golden Jubilee of Queen Victoria. It cost around £6,000 and was designed by Henry A. Cheers of Twickenham. In *Kelly's Directory* of 1891 it was described as 'a handsome building of red brick and Bath stone dressing in the Renaissance style'. Nearly 100 years later, as fashions changed, it was described by Nikolaus Pevsner as 'Ludlow's bad luck', and was demolished in March 1986. The building on the right is Castle Lodge, built in about 1564 for Thomas Sackford, an official for the Council of the Marches. The cannon was Russian and a gift to the town from the Government in 1857. Note that on days when the Market was not using Castle Square it was a park for the country buses.

The magnificent timber-framed building was erected at the beginning of the 17th century, narrowing quite considerably the junction where King Street, Broad Street and the High Street meet. Bodenhams moved their business to these premises in 1900 from another shop in King Street. On their awning they are advertising 'men and boys wear, town and country and school outfits'. On the left is the newsagents founded by Charles Cobbin at the beginning of the 20th century. Arthur Bessell, a wholesale and retail glass, china and earthenware dealer, occupied the house next door with the Regency-style bow windows. George Pearce, a fishmonger, who also traded in fresh fruit, vegetables and game, traded from the building at the end. Later J.P. Wood of Craven Arms bought the business. Note the milk bar and Carpenter's butcher's shop on the right and the errand boys' bikes with their front carrier, parked by the pavement.

This fine view of Ludlow was taken off the Whitcliffe, *c.*1930. Dominating the skyline is the lofty tower of the parish church of St Laurence, which was described by the writer John Leland in the 16th century as 'very fayer and large, and richly adorned, and taken for the fayrest in all these quarters.' In the foreground are the gardens below Dinham and Camp Lane. The large white house to the left with the entrance porch and the conservatory at the side is Dinham Lodge, which was built in about 1800. The building to the right with the white turret in the centre of the roof contains part of a chapel erected in the 12th century and dedicated to St Thomas Becket.

Dinham Bridge crosses the River Teme below the castle and was built in 1825 to replace a wooden structure erected on stone piers in around 1540. The bridge consists of three arches and has half columns above the watercuts. The buildings just beyond the bridge are part of a small industrial estate that contained a water mill, brass foundry and iron foundry. Hidden by the undergrowth on the right is a mill leat and arch beneath the bridge, which provided water for the mill and was designed by Thomas Telford. The name Dinham is probably derived from the Frenchman Joce de Dinan, who owned land in Ludlow in the 12th century. One of the footpaths near the bridge is known as Bread Walk.

This is a view of Mill Street taken from the Whitcliffe. The street takes its name from Ludlow's first water mill, which was destroyed by a flood towards the end of the 19th century. It was a corn and fulling mill and the remains of the sluice gates can be seen to the right of the weir. Lower Mill street narrows quite considerably by the top telegraph post, which is the site of Mill Gate, which cut through the town wall. The building on the right with the clock tower in Upper Mill Street is a 14th-century house built for Sir Hugh Cheney, which became the town's grammar school in 1527.

This is a fine view of the entrance to Ludlow's Butter Cross, looking towards King Street. The Corporation built it in 1743 on the site of the New House, an old timber-framed building erected in about 1570. The main entrance is in the centre of the building through an open porch supported by four Tuscan pillars. The open ground floor was used as a market for the sale of butter and other farm produce. The Blue Coat Charity School reopened in the upper room of the market in 1785 with 45 pupils on roll. At the end of the 19th century a group of clergymen led by the Revd E. Clayton set up a well-attended Working Men's Evening Club there. The architect of the market was William Baker of Audlem in Cheshire and it cost about £1,000.

Newton was a small settlement on the eastern side of the A49 and south of the crossroads leading north to Shrewsbury, south to Ludlow and Hereford, west to Clun and Bishop's Castle and east to Much Wenlock and Bridgnorth. In the middle of the 19th century the settlement was absorbed into the new town of Craven Arms in an area at the southern end of Market Street near the school and the Stokesay Hotel. The building on the right is a section of the Lion or Red Lion Inn that had been in operation since at least 1768. Around 1898 the licence was transferred to the newly opened Stokesay Castle Hotel and the old building was demolished in the 1920s. On the opposite side of the road below the timber-framed building is the premises of Thomas Griffith, the carpenter and wheelwright, who according to his sign was also the local painter and decorator. The timber-framed house is still there with its massive chimneystack, which is thought to be part of a tower used as a lookout post during the Civil War.

This photograph, taken in the 1950s, shows just how quiet the main A49 was at this time, with just three cyclists riding abreast of each other in the direction of Church Stretton. Just behind the war memorial is the yard belonging to Clifford Gough, a monumental mason. The large building to the left of the houses is the post office that was there from around 1940 until 1974, and just above is the Regal Cinema that opened in 1935. There was another Regal Cinema in Church Stretton and both belonged to the Craven Cinema Ltd and were known as the 'Luxury Cinemas of South Shropshire'. They were advertised as air conditioned and not just ventilated. The seating was luxurious with generous leg-room, which was far in excess of the regulations. The car and cycle park and cloakrooms were free and if you were hard of hearing a deaf aid was also supplied free of charge.

This is Market Street in Craven Arms, looking south in about 1950. The shops on the right belong to the Miller family. The ladies are standing outside the premises of Walter Miller, who was originally a house furnisher but later changed to selling bicycles. The grocery shop belonged to Mrs Martha Miller, who moved there at the beginning of the 20th century after establishing her business around the corner in Dale Street in 1898. The house with the army recruiting sign over the front door is Bristol House on the corner of Dale Street. Around 1895 it was the town's post office run by Edwin Thomas, who was also a local corn dealer. The house was later used as offices for auctioneer, valuer and estate agent Charles Edwards, before becoming Mrs Edwards' Refreshment Rooms. The notice inside the door announces the sale of teas, luncheons and snacks. The building at the bottom of the road is the Stokesay Castle Hotel.

A rainy day in Market Street in around 1930 makes a very dismal scene and would be unlikely to attract tourists to the area. The card was sent by Ethel, whose house was in Milwaukee Terrace on the Clun Road in Craven Arms, to Miss M. Wright in Buxton, Derbyshire. She informs her that 'the weather still keeps very cold' and that 'Mother was very poorly on the Sunday after we came home.' The large building on the right with the arcade is the Market Hall, which was built in 1888 with markets being held there every Friday. At the beginning of the 20th century the newsagents and booksellers W.H. Smith had opened a kiosk at the railway station with Charles Egginton as clerk in charge, but by the the time World War One broke out they had opened this shop in Market Street. Note the sign for Mrs Edwards' Dining Rooms: she later moved to Bristol House on the corner of Dale Street.

The school and the Stokesay Castle Hotel stand on a site that was once part of the hamlet of Newton. The first National School was built near Stokesay Church in 1858 and was enlarged in 1886 to accommodate 162 children. With the rapid growth of the town, and after a series of critical reports by the school inspector, a School Board with five members was formed in October 1892 and four years later this new school was opened to cater for 337 children. The Stokesay Hotel at the junction of Market Street and Newton Street was erected on land belonging to the Allcroft family and was run by Richard Hartshorn. The licence for the hotel was transferred from the old Red Lion that stood close by. By the 1930s the hotel was listed as a family and commercial hotel run by Mrs Helen Boulton, who advertised the following amenities: 'Tea Garden, First Class Tariff, Excellent Cuisine, Separate Tables, Electric Lighting, Every Comfort, Home From Home, Fishing, Golfing, Garage Adjoining, Cars For Hire. Tariff On Application.'

This view of Bishop's Castle was taken from the tower of the church and shows how Church Street bends round into the High Street and up to the Town Hall. Sir Richard Colt Hoare stayed at the Castle Hotel while visiting the town in June 1799. He recorded in his diary, 'I found a comfortable inn. The inn, its garden and the bowling green above it occupy the space of the Bishop's castle – here the Bishop formally resided til about the time of Q. Elizabeth. The town is a borough commanded by Lord Clive – dreary and dull – the ground around it is uncommonly rich and valuable – owing probably to the quantity of manure running down on it from the town on all sides. (Inn Good).'

A man speaks to three men on the opposite side of Bishop's Castle High Street one lunchtime in the 1930s. Dominating the view is the Town Hall, with its clock and bell tower, which was erected around 1765. It was built on the site of an older hall that was considered to be in a 'ruinous state' in 1615. The first floor was built as a council chamber and committee room while the ground floor was built to house the market. According to *Kelly's Directory* for 1929 market day was on a Friday 'for the supply of a wide agricultural district'. The building on the right with the arched doorway is the Midland Bank, while the building jutting out into the pavement above is Barclays Bank.

This is Church Street in Bishop's Castle, looking down towards the church. The people on the left are standing outside the Kings Head public house, which was occupied by the Pugh family for several generations between the 1860s and the 1930s. The inn had been fully licensed since 1832 and in 1900 was owned by the Revd William Bishton Garnett-Botfield, who lived at Decker Hill, Shifnal. The landlord was John Pugh, who was reported as a good manager, running a fair house, mainly for customers in the agricultural trade. The girl on the right is standing to the side of Red Lion Shut, which runs through to Union Street. The name commemorates an old inn that stood at this end of the passage but had gone by 1921. The shop to the right of the horse and cart is a grocer's shop belonging to George Owen, while just beyond, behind the wooden gate, is Morray's grocery and baker's shop.

The building in the centre is the old Market Hall in the Market Square at Bishop's Castle. It was built in the second half of the 18th century and was later used as a reading room and known as the Powis Institute. There were 70 members in 1905 and for a fee they were able to peruse a supply of daily newspapers and periodicals. The local lodge of Oddfellows also met in one of the rooms there. The building was demolished in 1951 but the Powis coat of arms over the top window has been preserved in the Square. The arms contain the figure of an elephant to commemorate Lord Clive's achievements in India. The agricultural implements in front of the hall belong to Arthur Greenhous, a local ironmonger, whose shop was just to the right. The shoe shop on the left belonged to George Cook and was established in the 1850s, while the shop on the right with the awning is Bradley's clothes shop.

The cottages on the right with the gabled second-storey windows and roofs finished off with unusual fish-scale tiles are in Welsh Street in Bishop's Castle. The photographer is looking back towards the town centre with the bell turret of the Market Hall just visible at the end of the road. The town once belonged to Egwin, a Saxon lord, who gave it to Hereford Cathedral after he had received a cure from the tomb of St Ethelbert. A Bishop of Hereford then built a castle at the top of the town to protect his land and renamed the settlement Bishop's Castle. The name of Welsh Street also reminds us of the town's close proximity to the Welsh border.

The people of Bishop's Castle pose quite readily for the photographer at the top of the High Street. The young boy on the left by the Town Hall has moved and become a ghostly double image. The shop on the right advertising a variety of products including Pratt's Motor Spirit, Eley Cartridges, Royal Daylight Lamp Oil and Raleigh and Singer Cycles is the ironmongers belonging to Edward Davies. Even at the beginning of the 20th century people had to deal with a different type of road pollution, as seen between the two police officers in the centre.

Church Street in Bishop's Castle *c.*1900 and not a car in sight. On the left an old man has a rest on his handcart before attempting to push it up the steep gradient of the High Street. This area of Bishop's Castle was once used as a cattle market before it was moved behind the Kings Arms. The building on the extreme left is the Six Bells public house, which was owned by the Earl of Powis and was first recorded in 1750. The white house above is Norton House, which was once used as a workhouse before Stone House, the Clun Union Workhouse, was opened in Union Street in 1840. The large house opposite with the impressive windows and stone balustrade on the roof is Lyme House.

Union Street in Bishop's Castle slips off from Church Street and runs almost parallel with High Street until they both meet at the Market Square. The street takes its name from the Clun Union Workhouse, built in the middle of the 19th century and demolished 100 years later to make way for a small hospital and residential home for the elderly. The old workhouse was known as Stone House and was often visited by vagrants travelling between workhouses, wanting overnight accommodation. At Stone House they had to earn their keep before they were given a meal and a bed, by breaking up a quantity of stone for use on roads. In 1901 the population of the town was 1,378, which included the five officials and the 50 inmates at the workhouse.

Taffy from Bishop's Castle sent this card to Mrs Pettifer of Broad Street, Bromyard, to ask if she knew anyone on the photograph, but unfortunately he doesn't tell us who they are. They are standing outside the cottages in Castle Street. Part of the site of the old castle, built in about 1127, is on the right, but very little of the original structure remains. A piece of the castle wall can be seen from Castle Street, but the site of the motte and bailey is now occupied by the bowling green. Just around the corner was another of the town's old inns, the Cross Keys.

There has been human activity in the area around Clun for over 5,000 years. There was a Bronze Age settlement near the site and the Saxons had a thriving community here before the arrival of the Normans. The town prospered, and in the 14th century it received a royal charter allowing it to hold a weekly market and two annual fairs. The prosperity of the town declined in the 19th century because the railway passed it by. The photographer is looking over the River Clun and up Bridge Street towards the town. The smaller white house with the bay window to the left of the bridge was a shop belonging to Mrs Betsy Jones, while opposite is the forge of blacksmith Richard Luther.

The Six Bells Inn on the right stood at the corner of Church Street and Vicarage Road in Clun until January 1915 when it burnt down. The landlord in 1905 was John Roberts, who was also listed as a monumental mason. By the look of the barber's pole you could also have your hair cut and enjoy a glass of beer at the same time. Once there were three other public houses standing in Church Street, the Two Chances Inn just below the Six Bells and the Crown Inn and the Bridge or Mason's Inn on the opposite side of the street. To battle against the evils of drink, the Temperance Hotel was built on the right next to the bridge at the bottom of the bank.

The photographer is looking over the rooftops of Church Street in Clun to the vicarage and church, which is dedicated to St George. Despite its village atmosphere, Clun is a small market town. As early as 1272 a weekly market was held there on a Tuesday and two fairs took place annually. The number of fairs was later extended to six, and these were held on the last Friday of the month in January, March, June, August, September and November. A hiring fair for servants was also held each year on 11 May. Until the middle of the 19th century Clun prospered, but after the railway had passed it by and larger towns like Ludlow, Church Stretton and Craven Arms became more accessible to the surrounding villages, its fortune waned. In 1881 Miss E. Neary wrote, 'If a spirit of enterprise was shown, Clun might be a most attractive place. Its situation is healthy and salubrious and would well repay visitors for a short sojourn in it. The spirit of improvement has not kept pace with the times'. Miss Neary's words have been listened to, as today Clun is an attractive centre that people want to visit.

The Town Hall at Clun was erected in the Square in 1780 by the second Lord Clive, who later became Earl of Powis. Material from the old Court House was used to build the hall and the Powis coat-of-arms can be seen over the doorway. The ground floor was originally open and still has its original cobbled floor. On fair days part of it was used as a gaol where prisoners were chained to iron rings sunk into the ground. Today the upstairs is a meeting room while downstairs is a small town museum. On the right is the post office and next door is the shop of John Clee the draper. The road to the right leads into the High Street.

This is a closer view of the Town Hall in Clun and the Powis coat-of-arms over the main door. The animal to the left of the crest is an Indian elephant, linking Lord Clive with India. The shop on the right belonged to William Mead, a grocer, ironmonger and oil and seed merchant who also ran a cycle and accessory store. Behind the hall on the left was a grocer's shop run by Charles Meredith. He was also a wine and spirit merchant, a draper and outfitter and a farmer at the Castle Grounds. Clun was always a busy little place and full of trade. Note the adverts for Cadbury's Chocolate and Cocoa and Colman's Starch by the shop on the junction of Bridge Street and the High Street and also the Clun Valley bus at the end of the road.

The High Street in Clun was once known as Frog Street. The white building on the left was the home and the maltings belonging to Joe Luther. In the middle of the 19th century the malt house facing the High Street was an inn called the Old Talbot. Two businesses were run from the shop on the right, owned by Thomas Williams. He was a saddler (note the horse collars by the left-hand window) and his wife and daughter were milliners (note the hats in the right-hand window). The men by the baskets look like street traders and are standing at the junction with Bridge Street.

The people on the left are probably waiting for the Clun Valley bus that used to pick passengers up at this point. The dog on the right is standing outside Sherwood's butcher's shop, while the lady in the centre is walking towards the North and South Wales Bank. At the beginning of the 20th century the bank was only open on Tuesdays between 11am and 2pm and on fair days; it was backed by the London Westminster Bank but was later incorporated into the Midland Bank. On the left is John Clee's draper's shop, next is the post office that was occupied for many years by Mrs Jessie Cooke, and at the top is the Buffalo Hotel with its smart inn sign and wonderful array of vehicles outside.

Clun Bridge was built in about 1450 and is a rare example of a complete mediaeval bridge. It is built out of stone and has five arches. The cutwaters on either side of the bridge also make a safe refuge for people travelling on foot as larger vehicles pass over. This view does not show the acute angle of the approach from this side of the bridge, which causes modern traffic so much trouble. The old saying about crossing the bridge will sharpen your wits would apply more to today's motorists than to drivers from the past. A reinforced saddle of concrete was used to strengthen the bridge in 1982 but the work cannot be seen and has not altered the appearance of the bridge. The building on the left, which lies at the foot of Church Street, is the Temperance Hall, built in 1870.

This is a very early photograph of Church Street in Clun, taken in the middle of the 19th century. The bridge is at the bottom of the hill but most of the buildings on the right were demolished within a few years of this photograph being taken. The timber-framed house was removed to make way for the Temperance Hall that was built in 1870. The white building on the right, which is still standing today, is the Two Chances Inn, which was delicensed before 1885. Higher up on the left are the steps leading into the Crown; another inn known as either the Mason's Arms or the Bridge Inn stood at the bottom of the bank on the same side.

This view of Church Stretton was taken from the side of Hazler Hill in the first half of the 20th century. The Shrewsbury to Hereford railway line is in the foreground, while the flat tops of the Long Mynd dominate the rear of the town. To the right, just above the tree line, are the new houses on Trevor Hill and above them is the clubhouse belonging to the golf club. Dominating the centre of the photograph is the tower of the parish church, which is dedicated to St Laurence. Today, most of the open land in the foreground has been built on.

This is a view of Church Stretton looking down the High Street from the Shrewsbury Road. The High Street was once the main north to south route through the town and was known as the Bristol Road. The turning to the left is Sandford Avenue, with Burway Road to the right. With the rapid growth of the town at the beginning of the 20th century banks were keen to get established in the town. Lloyds Bank acquired the site on the corner of Sandford Avenue and the High Street, while the Midland Bank occupied the corner of Burway Road. The building on the extreme left is the Hotel.

This is Burway Road in Church Stretton, looking towards Burway House at the top and the Long Mynd. Burway House dates from about 1778. A free school was founded there after Thomas Bridgman left a charity of 40 shillings a year in his will to pay a schoolmaster to teach four poor children, 'til they could perfectly read the Bible'. When the elementary school opened in 1861, Burway House became the home of Samuel Harley Hough, a solicitor. At the beginning of the 20th century it became a boys' boarding school, known as the Collegiate School. It then became a dentist's surgery and has since been changed into flats. The monument was a drinking fountain erected to commemorate Queen Victoria's Diamond Jubilee in 1897. It was moved a few years later to a site in front of Burway House, where it remained until 1963 when it was taken down after being hit by a large vehicle. The original site of the fountain is now occupied by the HSBC Bank, which took over the Midland Bank.

Sandford Avenue in Church Stretton takes its name from the Revd Holland Sandford, rector of Eaton-under-Haywood. At the top on the junction of Burway Road is the drinking fountain and beyond that Burway House. The building with the Hovis sign is on the corner of Easthope Road. It was a private and commercial hotel and a bakery, which was run by William Rees between 1905 and 1920. The round sign by the veranda advertises refreshments at the Stretton Café and in the window another sign announces Tea and Luncheon Rooms. Mrs Marion Evans, who was listed as a china dealer in 1917, occupied the building next door, but by 1921 she was also selling antiques. By 1929 the premises were occupied by her son John, who was a jeweller but also continued to deal in antiques.

A young lady rides side-saddle on her pony down the High Street in Church Stretton. The building on the left is the town hall, built in 1839 for about £1,000. It was a square building of red brick with a stone dressing, supported on stone pillars. A contemporary account considered the building as 'neither beautiful to the eye nor with any pretensions to architectural excellence'. It was demolished in about 1962 after it was found to be unsafe. The white building is the Plough, which was owned by R.B. Benson of Lutwyche Hall but leased to Southam's Brewery in Shrewsbury. It closed in January 1948 and its licence was transferred to the Sandford Hotel. On the right is Salt's ironmonger's shop with its fine frontage built out of Ruabon brick.

Church Stretton has always been a busy and bustling market town, especially on the Thursday market day. At the top of the High Street at the crossroads is the Hotel. The group on the left with the two girls in smart hats and wearing sailor collars are outside the Plough Inn. The window of the shop across the road is full of ladies' clothing but the sign on the awning is advertising Arthur Pope, a house decorator. He was also a glazier, plumber and hot water fitter, who guaranteed good work at moderate prices. He is housed in a building that was erected in about 1660 for Edward Berry, a solicitor. It later became the Lion Inn. Harry Boulton occupied the shop next door. He was a fishmonger and poultry dealer who had started his business in Sandford Avenue in around 1905. Just above is the shop of F. Baldwin and Son, who were butchers.

This is Sandford Avenue in Church Stretton, looking towards the railway bridge. Before it was renamed it was called Station Road, as the entrance to the railway station is the opening on the left just beyond the pavement. In the 19th century it was known locally as Lake Lane, as a brook in the area would flood the street after a heavy downpour. The large building by the trees on the right was built in about 1904 as a malt house. During World War Two it was converted into a canteen for troops and a workshop for St Dunstan's Hospital. The garage on the left was run by Henry Eastment and was called the Station Garage.

This view of Sandford Avenue in Church Stretton is looking back towards the town and the Long Mynd. On the left is the old post office building. At this period the post office is occupying the left-hand side of the building while George Dunn, a dispensing chemist, occupies the right-hand side. Mr Dunn also ran a stationery and fancy goods repository and a circulating library. The billboard outside his shop advertising the *Daily Mail* has the headline 'Crippen Inquest. Summing Up & Verdict'.

This is a rare view of Watling Street and Station Road in Church Stretton before the building of the bypass in 1939. The bridge on the right goes over the railway line into Sandford Avenue and the buildings just before the bridge are the only section of the Crossways development plan to be built. The plan that was first envisaged at the beginning of the 20th century was intended to move the shopping centre away from the town to an area close to the railway station. The complex was demolished in 1965 for a traffic island on the bypass that was never built. The shop on the corner is situated in Vernon House. In the 1920s Charles Wheatley occupied the grocery shop while his wife Ellen rented out some of the rooms in the house as apartments. The building was later converted into flats.

This area of Church Stretton lies to the south of the town and is known as World's End. It gave its name to a public house, which was originally called the Grapes. It was housed in the building with the large porch, which is situated on the bend of the road. The inn was first licensed in the middle of the 19th century and had become the World's End Inn by 1900. Martin Carter was landlord at this time and he was also listed as a fencing maker. Just above the inn is the gasometer belonging to the Stretton Gas Company. For many years Arthur de Zrinyi was the manger of the Gas Works. In his spare time he was also an accountant, assistant overseer and collector of rates and taxes, superintendent registrar of births, deaths and marriages, clerk to the Parish Council of All Stretton and Little Stretton, collector to the Urban District Council and an agent for an insurance company.

This view of Market Street in Craven Arms was taken at the beginning of the 20th century. The Stokesay Castle Hotel is at the bottom of the road. The children are standing in front of the shops belonging to the Miller family, who sold groceries and house furnishings. The building immediately behind the children and the open ground to the right were redeveloped into a smart new grocery store for the family in the 1920s. Other grocers in the town were George Rix and Giaus Smith, both companies having a number of other outlets in south Shropshire. The Shrewsbury and Wem Brewery and Southam's Brewery both had premises in Market Street, perhaps one of them in the building on the left with the advert for Bavarian Ales.

The beautiful countryside around Clun and the activities that take place there are extolled in this poem. It was written in the first half of the 20th century, as more people were starting to take recreational days and short holidays out into the beautiful hill country of south Shropshire.

A Summer Holiday at Clun

(WRITTEN BY REQUEST.)

1.—Of many places 'neath the sun
There are but few to equal Clun ;
So if you want a holiday
Pack up and start without delay.

2.—Broome Station is six miles away,
And Craven Arms is nine, they say,
A coach will take you up the Vale,
Past wood and meadow, hill and dale.

3.—And then, the six or nine miles done,
There comes in sight the town of Clun ;
The old Church Tower, the Castle Keep,
And in the distance, Rockhill steep.

4.—Fair Radnor Wood, and Guilden Down,
Bold Bury Ditches' dark green crown,
The Gallows-tree and Mowdens hill,
The Lake's smooth waters by The Mill.

5.—Then on the left, bleak Sowdley's plain,
The Rock, The Tongues, and Woodside Lane,
And nearer, Cwmshidie is seen,
The Hurst, the river, and The Green.

6.—One day we'll go to Offa's Dyke,
('Tis better far to walk than bike),
Descend from Spring-hill to The Spoad,
And back along Newcastle Road.

7.—Another day we'll climb Black Hill,
With " wimberries " ripe our baskets fill,
Where gorse and heather bloom and fade,
And changing bracken spreads its shade.

8.—Here will the artist love to stray,
The scholar too, both young, and grey,
Photographer, geologist,
Historian, and botanist.

9.—They one and all will something find
To please the eye, and charm the mind ;
The flush of health will fan the cheek,
And give fresh vigour to the weak.

10.—Farewell thrice happy Vale of Clun !
Our summer holiday is done ;
May all thy beauties long remain
To greet us when we come again.

R.H.

Chapter Two
Villages and Hamlets

Ashford Carbonell lies two miles south of Ludlow, close to the border with Herefordshire. The name is derived from the ford and the great ash tree that stood by it and the family name of the lord of the manor, William Carbonell. Locals believe that the first part of the name is derived from 'Asses Ford', a place where the old packhorses would have crossed the River Teme. The scene looks tranquil but in May 1907 a young boy named Davies was cycling through the village when a car carrying Dr and Mrs Downes came around the corner in the opposite direction. The cyclist ended up on the bonnet of the car while his bike was dragged several yards down the road beneath the vehicle. Dr Downes was involved in another crash a few months later when a car he was being driven in lost control on a bank at Hayton and turned over. The doctor and the driver were lucky as they escaped with some minor bruising.

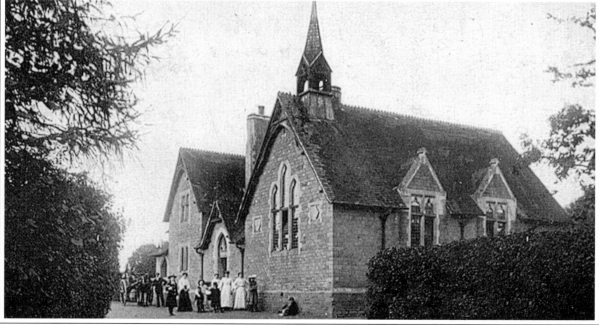

The school at Ashford Carbonell was built in a similar style to a Victorian church or chapel. It was a mixed school for infants, boys and girls, and was known as the National. It was erected out of brick with a stone dressing in 1872. The school was large enough to accommodate 100 children from the surrounding area, but in 1885 the average weekly attendance was 60. There was also a house for the mistress, who in 1885 was Miss Jeanette Kirby Cornock. Note the high windows, designed to stop the students from looking out and being distracted from their lessons.

The picturesque village of Bromfield stands at the confluence of the River Teme and the River Onny, a few miles north-west of Ludlow. Its name is derived from the golden broom that once flourished in the surrounding fields. The building with the signs on the side is the village post office that was run at the beginning of the 20th century by William Wadeley, the sub-postmaster and village tailor. Incoming mail reached the post office at 4.30am and outgoing mail left at 8.30pm. This view was taken from the bridge; note the entrance to the ford. Older residents of the village remember gypsy families camping out on the banks of the river for a short while to take part in horse-trading fairs.

Wistanstow is an Anglo-Saxon settlement, sited on an ancient crossroads. It takes its name from St Wystan, a Mercian prince. He was murdered in the village by an uncle or cousin who used a knife to slay him, while giving him the kiss of peace. There is a legend that from the place where his body fell a column of light, which lasted for 30 days, was seen ascending into the sky. It was also claimed that each spring, the hair cut off at the time of his death would spurt up like grass, attracting crowds of pilgrims to travel to the site. There have been many blacksmiths in the village; in 1871 the local smith was Thomas Williams, but by 1900 it was John Davies. From about 1917 William Reynolds was the village blacksmith and is probably the man in this photograph. In the early part of the 20th century alder trees were chopped down in the area and dragged into the village, where they would be cut and roughly shaped before being sent to clog makers up north.

The village of Onibury lies off the main A49 just five and a half miles north-west of Ludlow. Both the name of the village and the name of the Onny river that runs close by are thought to originate from the Welsh for ash trees. Although the history of the village goes back centuries, the village did not have its own public house until 21 December 1966. It was known as the Holly Bush, but it only had a short life and closed in around 1992. The main focal points for the village were the school that was built in 1871 and enlarged in 1893 and the village shop. Around 1900 the village shop was owned by Edwin Jones, who was also the local butcher and sub-postmaster. The post office received its mail from the sorting office at Craven Arms each morning at 7.15 and letters from the village were sent back at 6pm. By the 1950s the shop was owned by W.D. Price, who was able to advertise that 'Players Please' and 'Senior Service Satisfy' your smoking habit.

This nicely posed photograph of Wistanstow village was taken by one of the prolific photographers engaged by Wilding's printing firm to take images around the county so that they could reproduce them as postcards. The tower of the Holy Trinity Church can be seen on the skyline. Both the church and the tower date from the 12th century, but the top of the tower was rebuilt in around 1712. The children look as if they are about to set off for the school, which was situated near the church and opened in 1859 to accommodate 150 children. A master's house was built next door.

This is a view over the Bottom Bridge at Bucknell looking towards the Square. The girl is standing outside the Plough Inn with its sign hanging on the side of the house. In 1885 the proprietor was John Dodd, who advertised the Plough as 'One minutes walk from the Station on the Central Wales Railway, four-and-a-half miles from Knighton and about nine miles from the Craven Arms Junction. A good horse and trap for hire. Good stabling. Well aired beds'. The gate on the left leads into Smith and Sons' grocery shop. The bridge crosses the River Redlake that flows through the village. It has a span of 20ft, has two arches and is built out of brick and rubble masonry with flat coping stones on the parapet. The blurred lady on the right by the river seems to be filling a sack or basket.

The Redlake is usually a shallow running river that is easily forded and before the Bottom Bridge was built this was a natural crossing point. The thatched cottage on the left has been demolished. To the rear is the Railway Tavern and the little girl is standing outside Sherwood's butcher's shop. Charles Sherwood had been trading there from the 1860s and he was also listed as a beer retailer, probably running the Railway Tavern. He was still there in 1905 when *Kelly's Directory* recorded him as a butcher, beer retailer and farmer. His son Ernest succeeded him.

The lady and old gentleman are just crossing Church Bridge in Bucknell, named after the church of St Mary, which can be seen behind the trees on the left. It is an old arch structure and has a 22ft span. After a nasty accident involving a car and a horse, the bridge was widened by extending the arch with reinforced concrete and rebuilding the parapets with rubble masonry. The timber-framed house in the centre is Weir Cottage.

The area that runs along the side of the Redlake at Bucknell is known as the Causeway. In the distance, partially hidden by trees, is the church. The timber-framed building with the thatched roof on the left is Yew Tree Cottage, which was built on a stone base in the early 17th century. The roof was probably the work of local thatcher William Trow, but with the demise of local craftsmen the thatch on this building has been replaced by a tiled roof. The building on the right is the Old School House, the original village school until the new one was built in 1865. It was later converted into a general store and bakery where beautiful birthday cakes were made and displayed in the window until they were carried away for the birthday treat. The building dates from the early 17th century.

St Mary's School at Bucknell is named after the village church and it was opened in 1865. The school was built out of brick in a Gothic style with long high windows, allowing in lots of daylight for the pupils without allowing them a view of the outside world to distract them from their studies. The school was large enough to accommodate 100 children and in 1900 the average weekly attendance was 85. A master's house was built on the side of the school and was occupied by Henry Evans, the first headmaster, who was aged 24 when he took up the post. At first the school was supported by Mr Sitwell, the vicar, voluntary contributions and a grant of £8 16s 8d from the Davies and Grettons' charities. Extra teaching space and a kitchen were added to the school in 1966.

In the early part of the 20th century the village post office at Bedstone was operated by James Morris, who was also the local shopkeeper and blacksmith. The post office was only a small business, receiving and despatching letters via Bucknell, with the nearest money order and telegraph office three miles away at Leintwardine. Miss Dorothy Morris wrote the postcard to Miss J. Vaughn, who lived at The Narrow in Knighton. She informs Miss Vaughn that she enjoyed herself at a dance held at Brampton Bryan and that the postcard shows her home and her two small brothers.

The children pose quite shyly for the photographer in the village of Colebatch, a small hamlet that lies one and a half miles south of Bishop's Castle. 'Batch' is the local word for a stream or valley, and the prefix of the name could be derived from 'Cola', a Saxon personal name, giving the village the name of Cola's Stream or Valley. In the 12th century Lefwyn de Colebech, who took his surname from the area, owned the land. In 1900 the population was made up of farmers and their workers but there was a carpenter and a blacksmith living in the village. To go to school the children would have had to travel to Bishop's Castle.

The tiny hamlet of Stow lies in a secluded valley of the River Teme just one and a half miles to the north-east of Knighton and the Welsh border. The church of St Michael has a backdrop of fir trees at the rear, while ancient yew trees grow in the churchyard. The walls of the church date back to the 13th century, while its fine wooden roof was added in the 17th; the roof is topped by a wooden belfry and spire. The chancel window depicts the Ascension with lancet windows showing Faith and Hope. There are also two fine mosaics, one showing three child angels and one showing Faith on a golden background. The name of the village is often spelt as Stowe with an 'e'.

The village of Lydham is situated at a crossroads on the Bishop's Castle to Shrewsbury road, two miles north-east of Bishop's Castle. The name of the village is derived from the old English 'hlid' meaning a slope and 'ham' meaning a meadow by a stream. The church is dedicated to the Holy Trinity and was built in the 13th century but restored in 1642 and again in 1885. To the rear of the church lie the remains of a motte and bailey castle and a mediaeval mill. The houses on the left are named Lily and Violet Cottages and were built in 1900. The little thatched building next door has been replaced by another house called Rose Cottage.

The name Norbury is derived from 'North Fort'. The village is small and lies at the foot of Norbury Hill to the west of the Long Mynd. The Public Elementary School was founded in 1874. It cost over £2,500 and was paid for by money bequeathed by the late Mrs Scott of Stourbridge. It could easily accommodate 150 children. The building, with its lofty tower, is often mistaken for a church. Ten years after it was built it was described as, 'A building erected of Norbury and Bath stone, which forms an elegant feature in the plain, west of the Stretton hills, where it is conspicuous for a long distance, and is seen from the Craven Arms and Bishop's Castle line.' In 1885 it was being supported by Mrs Scott's son John, who was a big landowner in the area and had homes at the Manor House, Ratlinghope, and at 6 Cambridge Gate, Regent's Park, London.

The children of Lydbury North Public Elementary School pose for the photographer in about 1910. The village had two schools, one Church of England and one Catholic. The Church of England school was founded over 300 years ago after John Shipman gave £200 in 1662 'for and towards the maintenance of a free school in the Parish of Lydbury North.' The schoolmaster was to be chosen by the Walcot family and the first school was over their chapel in the south chancel of the church. A new school was built in the village in 1845 to hold 175 children.

The Catholic school was known as Plowden School and was opened in 1874. It was for many years supported by the Plowden family, who were staunch Catholics. It provided accommodation for 52 pupils but was enlarged in 1896, when a new classroom and two cloakrooms were added, increasing the accommodation to 79 children. The inscription on the gable end on the right says, 'W.F.P.1896'. The initials stand for William Francis Plowden. Although a Catholic school, many non-Catholics in the village used it to save the journey to school in Lydbury North. During World War Two the school was filled to overflowing with evacuee children from Birmingham and Liverpool. At the rear of the school to the left is the tower of St Walburga's Catholic Church, built in 1868. The church is still used but the school has closed and the buildings have been converted into cottages.

Hopesay is a small hamlet tucked away down a quiet valley two and a half miles west of Craven Arms. It is protected on either side by the Burrow and Wart Hills, which are both topped with Iron Age hill forts. The name of the village is derived from 'hop' meaning a valley and the name of the de Say family, who were the lords of the manor and owned a great deal of land in the area. Apart from the village shop, run by William Deane, the village was mainly inhabited by farmers and farm labourers at the start of the 20th century.

Edgton lies three and a half miles north-west of Craven Arms in the beautiful undulating countryside of south Shropshire. Several roads and footpaths converge on the village, showing that at one point in its history it was a place of some importance. There are a number of old stone and timber-framed buildings scattered around the village, but the church was rebuilt in 1895 leaving only the 13th-century windows surviving from the old structure. On the reverse of the card Rene informs Miss K. Marston of the Woodlands, Market Drayton, that she was having a good time there and that she had visited Craven Arms on the Saturday and attended a show and a dance.

Clunton is a pretty little village, which lies two and a quarter miles east of Clun. At the beginning of the 20th century most of the inhabitants were farmers and worked on the land but there was a marine store dealer, a water mill, the Crown Inn and the post office. The post office, which also incorporated the village shop, is situated in the building just across the bridge and was run by Mrs Sarah Morris. All mail was delivered through the post office at Aston-on-Clun, which was the nearest money order and telegraph office. The little two-arched bridge straddles the River Clun.

Clunbury lies at the foot of Clunbury Hill, four miles east of Clun. The children are standing outside the village post office and may be walking home from school as three of the boys are carrying satchels. In 1921 the sub-postmaster was Frederick Mold, who was also the collector of water rates for Clunbury and Clunton Rural District Council. For many years the Mold family were also the village blacksmiths. In the background is the tower of St Swithin's Church.

The children line up by the railings of Clunbury School, which was erected in 1862 along with a house for the master. In *Bagshaw's Directory* for 1851 it is recorded that the original Parish School was 'built on the waste, by subscription, and is partly supported by the rents of two closes of land.' This school was built for 112 pupils but it was enlarged twice, in 1893 and 1904, making room for 150 children, although the average weekly attendance in 1905 was 120. Mr and Mrs W.E. Deacon were the master and mistress there for many years in the late 19th and early 20th centuries. Mrs Deacon started as the sewing mistress but later looked after the education of the infants. The money subscribed to the school from the land rent was stopped in 1905.

Church Road in Clunbury has changed very little over the years, although the house behind the car has had the plaster removed and its timbers exposed. The cottage on the right was built in about 1556 and it is believed to have been an inn called the Pig and Whistle and later the Raven. In 2002 the building was extensively renovated. The dormer windows were raised and a third one was added and the whole roof was re-thatched and crowned with a straw bird and a stag, complete with a full set of antlers. A narrow thatched porch was put over the front door and the two bay windows. The church stands behind the wall on the left.

This Arbour Tree at Aston-on-Clun was an English or native poplar that stood on that site for about 300 years until it was blown over during heavy gales in 1995. This photograph, taken in the 1920s, shows the tree with some of its flags, which were hung on long larch poles and placed on the tree during a ceremony held each year on Oak Apple Day, 29 May. According to local folklore the flags commemorate the wedding of John Marston of Aston-on-Clun and Mary Carter of Sibdon, who were married on that day in 1786. Historians believe that the tradition is much older and dates back to Celtic times when women's clothing was hung on special trees during the planting season to ensure the fertility of the soil. A new poplar has been planted in the village and the tree dressing ceremony is still performed each year. The ladies with their luggage are waiting for the Clun Valley bus to pick them up.

From as early as the 17th century money and land has been donated to charities for the benefit of the poor people of Clungunford. In August 1718 £5 from the rental of land bought for £85 out of School Stock was paid for the hiring of a school teacher. In February 1748 another piece of land at Abcot was conveyed 'to the use and benefit of the said school and school master for teaching and instructing the children of every inhabitant of the said parish'. The following year another £50 was donated, 'upon condition that the children of all the inhabitants of Broome should be taught and instructed by the said school master in as beneficial a manner as the other children'. This school was erected with a house for the schoolmaster in 1855 to accommodate the needs of 128 children.

Newcastle-on-Clun is a village where the houses are built mainly out of stone. A church dedicated to St John the Evangelist was built in the Early English style in 1848 and two years later a school was erected for 100 pupils, partly supported by a yearly grant of £50 donated by Clun Hospital. In 1905 the village supported three grocers, two wheelwrights, a blacksmith, a dressmaker, a cobbler, the Crown Inn and a beer retailer. The Whitcott Road leads to Whitcott Keysett, a small village to the east.

This is the southern entrance into Little Stretton, the narrow little road once being the main route from Shrewsbury to Ludlow. Just beyond the cottages where the washing is drying used to be one of the three village shops. In the 1930s the village also supported two refreshment rooms, five boarding houses and three inns. One of the inns, the Green Dragon, can be seen at the end of the road. The inn had been fully licensed in 1818 and was owned and occupied in 1901 by Charles Davies. His house was reported to be clean and in good order, although his stables were under repair. His trade came from local farm workers, people passing and from boarding tourists.

The aptly named Brook Road in Little Stretton leads into Ashes Valley. On the right is the Old Tan House, which was erected in the 17th century and was once the home of Derwent Wood, the sculptor, who was responsible for restoring the house. In 1921 Capt. D.E. Macpherson, a local pig breeder, was in residence there. It later became the home of Lt-Col. Graham Howard Gwyther DSO of the Royal Welch Fusiliers. During World War One he was mentioned in despatches. He received his DSO in 1916 and was severely wounded. Before retiring in 1920 he commanded the 2nd Volunteer Company KSLI. On the other side of the road is Rose Cottage, which was the home of William Duckett, a painter and decorator. During the 1930s his wife Lucy opened a boarding house there.

The car is parked outside the Ragleth Inn at Little Stretton. Around 1900 there were three public houses in the village, the Green Dragon, the Sun and the Crown. The Crown closed and was converted into the village shop. The Green Dragon is still in existence but the Sun changed its name to the Ragleth sometime between 1905 and 1909, to commemorate the hill nearby. The cottages on the left are still known as The Ancient House. When this photograph was taken the timber-framed section was for sale through Jackson and McCartney, auctioneers, valuers and land and estate agents from Craven Arms.

Early records show that John Rawlins owned the village shop at All Stretton in 1849, when it was known as Stores Cottage. When it was sold to Samuel Heighway in 1899 the property was described as 'a dwelling house, shop, outbuildings and garden'. By 1917 Mr Heighway had gone into partnership with a Mr Humphreys and they opened other shops in Shrewsbury, Church Stretton and Baschurch. The company was particularly proud of its Indian and Ceylon teas, which were sold at 1s 10d or 2 shillings a pound. In an advert they claimed customers for their tea from 'all over England including London, also Paris, Dresden and Munich'. The business was sold in 1922 to Edward Davies, who in turn sold it to William Green two years later. Mr Green was advertised in 1937 as a family grocer, provisions dealer and a wine and spirit merchant. The family ran the store until 1968.

The village of Munslow lies on the main road from Craven Arms to Much Wenlock. Many of the cottages in the village have been built out of Wenlock stone. The church in the village is dedicated to St Michael and is a mixture of architectural styles, but dates back to Norman times. Inside the church there is a large stone from the Great Wall of China, brought home by a naval relative of a former vicar in 1884. The houses on the left have been extensively altered since this photograph was taken and have been given dormer windows.

The village of Cardington nestles among the hills of Willstone, Cardington, Lawley and Caer Caradoc, just four miles east of Church Stretton. The focal points of this view are the two main establishments of any village, the church and the village inn. The church is dedicated to St James and has a 12th-century nave and a 13th-century tower. In the chancel is a memorial to William Leighton, Chief Justice of North Wales and a member of the Council of the Marches. He lived nearby at Plaish Hall, which was built in about 1540. The village once supported two hostelries, the Royal Oak, which is still catering to the public, and the New Inn, which once brewed its own ale but is now converted into a private house. The children are posing around the pigsty belonging to the Royal Oak.

The village of Longden lies five miles south-west of Shrewsbury on the road from the county town to Bishop's Castle. The name of the village is derived from 'long hill' and at the time of the Domesday survey it was held by the Corbet family. The settlement was owned later by the Botterell family before being passed on to Robert Burnell in about 1282. Robert Burnell was Lord Chancellor of England and Bishop of Bath and Wells. He built a fortified manor as his home in Acton Burnell, seven miles south-east of Shrewsbury. At the beginning of the 20th century most of the inhabitants of the village worked on the land but there was also a farrier, a blacksmith, a horse slaughterer, two shops and two inns, the Red Lion and the Tankerville Arms. The post office is the first building on the left; the building behind the second bush has since been demolished.

This view was taken from the Brockton to Worthen road in Minsterley looking back over the bridge towards the Shrewsbury to Bishop's Castle road. The first bank to open in Minsterley was the London City and Midland Bank. Lloyds Bank on the left had opened this sub-branch by 1922 and carried out business on Fridays between 11.30am and 3pm. The dog is walking towards the village store, which was occupied for many years by the Roberts family. They sold a wide variety of goods, including tin baths, as displayed in front of the shop. The post office is housed in the next building and just beyond the telegraph pole is a newsagents and tobacconist's shop. It was later converted into a butcher's shop.

This view from Pontesbury Hill looks down to the church of St George, which is situated in the middle of Pontesbury. The chapel on the right has been converted into a house. In 1811 the people living on the hill were lucky as in May that year they would have missed the devastation caused by a great flood. The tragedy was caused by a violent storm that unleashed a huge cloudburst over the Stiperstones. The waters rushed down the valleys with irresistible force, sweeping away cottages, mills, cattle and trees. The depth of water in the village ranged between 13 and 17ft deep. Nine villagers were drowned during the flood.

Although many of the buildings in this photograph of Pontesbury are still there today, there have been a number of changes since it was taken at the beginning of the 20th century. The main difference is that the white building on the corner of Chapel Street has been demolished to give wider access into the road leading to Habberley. The building appears to be a shop of some kind. The house beyond and the cottages in Chapel Street are still there. The buildings on the right have hardly changed, but their small front gardens have been removed to allow better road access into the village. The photographer has his back to the Red Lion Inn, looking towards Shrewsbury.

Situated on the road from Bucknell to New Invention, in the valley of the River Redlake and surrounded by hills, is the tiny village of Chapel Lawn. The name is derived from a chapel attached to Chapel Lawn Farm in the 16th century and 'lawn' refers to a clearing in a forest. In the centre is the church of St Mary, which was designed by Edward Haycock senior of Shrewsbury in 1844. To the left of the church is Chapel Lawn School, erected in 1856 to accommodate 75 children at a cost of £478 2s 2d. By 1985 the number of children on roll had fallen to 16, leading to the school's closure at the end of the summer term. The remaining pupils were transferred to Bucknell School.

The old Toll House was built on the Minsterley to Brockton Road by the Bishop's Castle turnpike trust. The double-fronted building with its ogee windows on the ground floor and small rounded windows on the first floor is unusual and not a very functional design for a tollhouse. The house became derelict and was in danger of falling down but in recent years it has been sensitively restored. Two people by the name of Evans owned grocery shops in the Minsterley area at this time. One was Miss Edith Evans, while the other was Mr James Evans. The adverts outside the shop are for Oxo and Spratt's food. The shop has been demolished and the road widened to accommodate a mini island.

Broad Street in Chirbury leads down to a T-junction, the left-hand fork taking you to Montgomery while the right-hand fork takes you to Welshpool. The shop on the right with the smart porch at the front door and the awning belonged to Edward Powell, who was listed as a draper and a grocer and an agent for W. & A. Gilbey Ltd, wine and spirits merchants, whose sign can be seen hanging outside. Mr Powell was also the sub-postmaster, offering a full range of services including the distribution of mail that arrived at his shop by mail cart from Montgomery every morning at 5.35am.

This view of Chirbury was taken from the top of St Michael's Church tower, which stands on the site of an Augustinian priory. According to local folklore, if you walk 12 times around the church at midnight on Hallowe'en you will hear the names of those in the village who will die in the next 12 months. The village is a mixture of architecture, with many buildings erected out of red brick, interspersed with timber-framed and stone houses. The large building with the car outside is the Herbert Arms, the only public house in the village.

The mixed Public and Elementary School and teacher's house were built in Marton in 1864 for the education of 60 children. A storm of protest arose when the County Council closed the school in 1948. The villagers were so upset at the loss that they grouped together and reopened the school, paying the teachers £3 a week out of their own pockets. In 1951 the authorities relented and took charge of the school again until 1984 when the number of pupils on roll fell and the school was closed again. The school building has now been converted into a house. The Congregational church on the left was first opened in 1827 but rebuilt in 1873 with seating for 126 worshippers. The land for the church was large enough to include a graveyard.

Villagers pose for the photographer on a very wet and miserable day in Marton. The weather was completely different when R.E.P. sent this postcard to Miss L. Hitchener, informing her: 'The weather now is turning out lovely'. He also tells her he is just going to call at the Sun Inn on the right. Marton is the birthplace of Dr Thomas Bray, who began the Parish Libraries System that was developed into the Society for the Propagation of Christian Knowledge. In the US he founded the Society for Propagating the Gospels after being sent to Maryland by the Bishop of London.

Worthen is situated 13 miles south-west of the county town in the valley of the Rea Brook. On the right Joseph Lloyd stands outside his grocery shop and post office, which he occupied from about 1900 until the 1930s. He was also a coachbuilder and two of his vehicles stand opposite his shop. The buildings in the centre once housed a butcher's shop owned by Albert Bunce and the Kynaston Arms, which was advertised by the landlord William Downes in 1905 as 'a hotel with every accommodation for cyclists and tourists'. The inn took its name from the Revd W.C.E. Kynaston, a former owner who lived at Hardwicke. The village had a second public house called the White Horse.

This view of rural life in Worthen was taken in about 1900. The postcard was sent to Miss E. Edwards of 3 Park Street in Manchester by a girl called Liz, who gives us a lot of information on the scene. She writes: 'Dear Ethel, Thanks for your P.C. This is a view of the Back Lane, it has a finer name now, as you will see, do you remember Mrs Tom Lloyd she is the one with the apron on. The man is Alfred Speak and the girl without the hat is Alice Blakemore and the dog is our Tobby he is such a funny little fellow. I don't think you know any of the others. I will send you a view of the village next time. With love from Liz.' Alice Blakemore was the daughter of Edwin Blakemore, a stone mason, and the finer name for Back Lane was Hampton Road. The postcard was sent on 5 February 1906.

Brockton lies less than a mile to the south-west of Worthen and is one of the many hamlets that were dependent on the village when Worthen was seen as a town at the time of the Domesday survey in 1086. At the beginning of the 20th century Brockton had its own tailor, shoemaker, shop and public house called the Cock, which is situated just past the cottages behind the trees. It also had a water mill, one of three in the area using the waters of the Rowley and Tantree brooks as a source of power. Note the loading bay just to the left of the lorry and the Wem Ales sign on the prefabricated building behind the telegraph pole.

Since this photograph was taken of Dorrington in the early 1950s, the main A49 road, taking traffic south towards Ludlow, has been considerably widened at the southern end of the village. The Horseshoes Inn on the right has been a public house since about 1734. In 1896 the inn was owned by the Revd St Ledge Hope-Edwards of Netley Hall, but managed by Mrs Margaret Hotchkiss. The inn had two kitchens, a bar, a parlour, a commercial room, eight bedrooms and a cellar. There was a large stable at the rear with room for 12 horses. By the 1930s it was another inn that had been taken over by the People's Refreshment House Association Ltd and advertised as a hotel. The shop by the telephone box is the post office and stationers run by Mrs Annie Owen.

Great Ryton lies nearly a mile east of the A49, five miles south of Shrewsbury. The name is derived from the Anglo-Saxon for 'the settlement where the rye is grown'. The two village shops are both on this photograph. On the left, advertising Cadbury's chocolate and Royal Daylight lamp oil, is Edward Edwards' grocery shop. The other shop, belonging to Thomas Onions, is behind the lorry in the centre. He was a grocer, a baker and the sub-postmaster, running the business there for many years. In around 1900 a ladies' boarding school was situated in the village at Ryton Fields and was organised by the Principal, Mrs J.W. Hoult.

The entrance into the village of Longnor was completely altered in 1925 when this bridge replaced the old footbridge and ford. The new bridge is built out of reinforced concrete to a design known as a 'multi box culvert'. It is functional and gives easier access into the village but is not as picturesque as the old view. There are stories of a ghostly figure of a young girl wearing a wedding dress haunting the area around the bridge; she has also been sighted at village dances. The house on the left is Bank House, which was once the home of Edmund Taylor.

Leebotwood lies 10 miles south of the county town as you approach the Stretton Hills. This view is looking north towards Shrewsbury and shows four of the six council houses built at the end of the village between 1926 and 1928. The building on the right with the fine thatched roof and the two cars parked outside is the Pound Inn. The inn is reputed to be the oldest house in the village and was built as a two-bayed cruck-framed building with a 17th-century boxed-framed solar at the southern end. At the beginning of the 19th century it was a farmhouse, but it was converted into an inn after the old hostelry at the northern end of the village was burned down. The man on the left could be a travelling salesman. He is smartly dressed, has two suitcases by his feet, and is holding some of his sample wares.

Castle Pulverbatch lies on the main road between Shrewsbury and Bishop's Castle about nine miles south-west of the county town. In 1900 the population were mostly farmers and farm labourers, but there was a tailor, a blacksmith, a village shop and two inns, the White Horse on the left and the Woodcock. The side road leads up to Huglith Hill and the tiny settlement of Westcott. The well-preserved earthworks of a motte and bailey castle remain on the left of the road. The castle is first mentioned in 1183 when Herbert de Castello occupied it. He acquired it as part of his marriage settlement to Emma de Pulverbatch. The castle was still habitable until the 15th century.

The timber-framed building is the White Horse Inn at Castle Pulverbatch. The road running past the inn is a minor road climbing up to Huglith Hill. The main road to Shrewsbury passes the little girl and the man while the road to Bishop's Castle drops to the right. The buildings to the right of the White Horse are a pair of cottages, the village shop, which was run in 1900 by Mrs Sarah Jones, and the Woodcock Inn. The Woodcock was first licensed in 1821 and was named after the owner, W.S. Woodcock, who lived in Churton. In 1901 the inn consisted of a bar, a parlour, two kitchens and four bedrooms. The landlord was John Phillips, who brewed his own beer.

Church Pulverbatch lies just off the main Shrewsbury to Bishop's Castle road about three quarters of a mile from Castle Pulverbatch, which with the hamlets of Cothercott, Wilderley and Wrentnall makes up the larger parish. Church Pulverbatch has been known locally as Churton since the 13th century and is the site of the parish church. The Welsh destroyed the first church in 1414. Most of the present building dates from 1854 but the tower is older and was erected in about 1773. Apart from the inns, Churton had all the main facilities including the Public Elementary School, built for 81 children in 1873, and the post office, run in 1900 by Mrs Eliza Bowen, who was also listed as a draper.

Pontesbury has always been one of the larger villages of the county but since the 1950s it has grown into a dormitory settlement for the surrounding area. The council houses in the centre were some of the first to be built and they have been followed by a number of private housing estates. The large shop and bakery in the foreground belonged to Edwin Bennett, who established his business in the village at the beginning of the 20th century. The area has recently been redeveloped and new housing built on the site, which is known as 'The Old Stores'. The car on the corner by the timber-framed building has stopped outside the village garage. In 1937 there was only one garage in the village and it belonged to John Hughes. He was advertised as an automobile, electrical, motor and general engineer. You could also obtain petrol from the road side pumps, hire a car or have your accumulator charged there.

With very little traffic on the road in the late 1920s people in Pontesbury were able to walk down the centre of School Bank in comparative safety. A school has existed in the village since the 16th century. It was placed under the control of the National Society in 1821 and by the 1850s the average attendance was about 100 children. In 1854 the rector described the school buildings as 'damp, low, ill-ventilated and ready to fall to the ground'. A new school to accommodate 200 pupils was erected on the right in 1855 at a cost of £900. The old school was converted into the master's house until it was demolished in 1875 and replaced by an extension for infants. This school was demolished in 1965 after a replacement had been built in Linley Avenue. The grocery shop and houses on the left are still there. Walter Davies started the shop around the corner in a wooden shed in about 1921. In the 1930s the shop was advertised as a parcel centre for the Midland Red Bus Company, which was carrying on the tradition of the old country carriers by collecting and delivering packages to the outlying villages of the county.

Chapter Three
Working Life

Under the shadow of Ludlow Castle the local labourers gather in the hay. The postmark on the postcard is timed and dated 8pm on 16 July 1908 and the view could depict the harvest of that or the previous year. The harvest of 1907 was good, and the hay harvest was the largest single crop and the most valuable raised in the country. The difference between a good harvest and a bad harvest had a great effect on the prosperity of the nation. The quantity of hay harvested in the previous 10 years varied between 11½ million tons and 16 million tons and was worth 40s a ton in 1907. In 1909 the cost of haymaking was 3s 6d per acre, but scenes like this were beginning to disappear, as fewer labourers were needed in the fields as farming became more mechanised.

This photograph was taken from Ludford Bridge, looking down to the 'Horse-shoe Weir', which powered watermills on both sides of the river. The mill on the left is the Old Street Mill, which was erected on this site in about 1331. It was known as the New Mill to distinguish it from the one in Mill Street that was known as the Old Mill at this time. In 1610 the mill was leased to William Gregory at a rent of 53s 4d. He proceeded to rebuild the mill and in 1620 erected a second mill on the same site. The mill in this view was built in 1810 from plans drawn up by Thomas Telford.

This is a trade postcard printed as a joint project by Frederick Wheeler Barnes, a butcher, and Smith and Co. Supply Stores of Corvedale Road, Craven Arms. Mr Barnes was there from around 1900 to about 1918. He seems to have a tremendous amount of stock on display for the photographer. Note the patriotic sign 'Roast Beef of Old England' hanging in front of the carcasses. Smith & Co. are a branch of Gaius Smith & Co., whose head office was in Ludlow. They had other branches in Clun, Bishop's Castle, Stottesdon and Church Stretton in south Shropshire, as well as Tenbury and Leominster in Herefordshire and Presteigne and Knighton across the border in Wales. As well as grocers they were bakers and confectioners and sold a great deal of household goods. On the reverse of this card Mr Barnes writes to Mrs East of Hopesay on 24 June 1907: 'Madam, I beg to say that your order for Pickled Beef shall be delivered on Tuesday June 25. Yours Obediently F.W. Barnes'.

The town of Craven Arms grew up around the railway, with the line between Shrewsbury and Ludlow being formally opened on 21 April 1852. The *Salopian Journal* described the new station at Craven Arms as a 'large and commodious station, in the Elizabethan style of architecture, with pointed gables, a large booking office, ladies' and gentlemen's waiting rooms, an excellent residence for the station master, railway and road weighing machines, sidings, turntables and platform of 170 feet in length, cattle landing 200 feet, goods warehouse 80 feet by 40 feet, coal wharf etc.' In 1870 a refreshment room with a full licence was opened on the down side of the station. It was owned by the Joint Railway Companies but occupied by George Hyles, the owner of the Clarendon Hotel in Shrewsbury. The train passing through the station ran between Craven Arms and Wellington via Much Wenlock and is being pulled by a Great Western tank engine.

Broome is a tiny hamlet lying close to the village of Hopesay. In the middle of the 19th century it was fortunate to be on the route of the new Central Wales Line that was being built by the London and North Western Railway company from Craven Arms through to Builth Wells and on to Swansea. Broome was the first station after Craven Arms and other larger settlements in the area like Clun were disappointed that they had been passed by. The buildings were made out of wood. The tall one on the left is the signal box with the main station building on the right containing the ladies' and gentlemen's waiting rooms and parcel and ticket offices. Behind the station was a siding containing a goods shed and loading yard. The line was due to close in 1963 but protests from the public kept it open.

At the beginning of the 20th century there were two shops in Bucknell, one belonging to Mrs Elizabeth Picken and this one belonging to Smith and Sons. Smith's was the larger and sold a wide variety of groceries and other items. Note the adverts for Colman's starch and mustard and the large Brasso sign by the door. The windows are also packed with a fine array of goods and, judging from the tiles on the roof, the shop may have been enlarged to cope with all the stock. The Smiths were trading in the village from about 1890 until the second half of the 20th century. The men on the photograph, left to right, are: Mr Smith, Sam Burgoyne (roundsman), Tom Passant (baker), George Smith and Frank Smith.

There have been two water mills on the River Redlake as it runs through Bucknell. One was called the Upper Mill while the other was called the Lower Mill. Both mills were close together and both in their history have been called the Old Mill, which often led to confusion. This is the Lower Mill, which was run by John Mason at the time of the Tithe Apportionment in 1839. John Mason was still there in 1851 and both mills were in operation, but just five years later Mason had gone and only one mill is listed.

The man in the pony and cart waits patiently at the level crossing for the engine to leave Bucknell Station and make its way towards Craven Arms. The pony and trap on the left are parked outside the entrance to the booking office and the wooden building behind the engine is the signal box. The new Central Wales Line opened in 1863, taking traffic from Craven Arms down through Knighton and Builth Wells and on to Swansea. The new line gave the villagers access to all parts of the country, altering their lives quite considerably. Keeping a sharp eye on the proceedings is the local policeman, the mainstay of law and order until the village constable was taken away in 1963.

A tank engine heads the train entering Bucknell Station and is possibly the Thursday Special returning to Builth Wells. The main station building on the right is one of the finest on the line, being built out of rough stone with a polychrome roof and elaborate gables. The ones on the left give access to the booking office and waiting rooms. In the early days the station gave employment to a number of villagers, with two sets of staff on duty to deal with either passenger or goods traffic. Today the station is unmanned and deals with only passenger traffic.

This view is looking over the level crossing at Bucknell and down the road leading from the village towards the A4113 to either Leintwardine or Knighton. The end of the main station building is on the right and just beyond the house on the left is the entrance to the goods depot and coal yard. When the railway first opened, new industry was attracted to the area, dealing with timber and bark. Local farmers were also able to transport sheep and cattle further and more easily than before and the Radnor Coal Company opened a coal depot in the yard. By the middle of the 20th century the line was threatened with closure but after huge protests it was kept open for passengers, although the goods traffic that had brought prosperity to the village ceased. On several occasions engines have smashed through the gates of the level crossing when signal box staff have failed to open them for an incoming train.

Bucknell post office opened in this building in the early 20th century. In 1885 mail arriving and leaving the village was dealt with by James Everall, the receiver, who was based at the railway station. All letters had to have RSO added to the address, which stood for Railway Sub-Office. Letters arrived at the station at 7.30am and the outgoing mail went at 8.10pm. The nearest money order and telegraph office at this time was at Knighton. By 1900 the post office was still at the station and was being run by Miss Martha Everall, the sub-postmistress, who could issue money orders and postal orders but could not cash them. The nearest telegraph service was still two miles away in Brampton Bryan. By 1905 William Watson Sherwood had become sub-postmaster and within a few years had moved into this building.

This building became the post office in about 1919 after alterations made by the new sub-postmistress Mary Picken. The shop also sold groceries and a variety of goods including clothes, hats and footwear that can be seen in the left-hand window. The buildings on the right belonged to her husband and were used as a garage and bicycle repair shop. Mr Picken was advertised in the 1920s as 'Motor and General Engineer, Repairers of Oil and Petrol Engines, Cycles and Accessories for Sale.'

The first section of the Bishop's Castle Railway was opened on 1 February 1866 and it was hoped that the line would travel on to Montgomery and from there to the Welsh coast. The line, which covered around 18 miles, left the main line just above Craven Arms and had stations at Horderley, Plowden, Eaton, Lydham Heath and finally Bishop's Castle. The plan was for the line to continue from Lydham Heath through Hyssington and Chirbury to join the Cambrian line just outside Montgomery. The line to Bishop's Castle, measuring a mile and a half, was just a spur with trains reversing there from Lydham Heath. The platform and the main Bishop's Castle station buildings are on the right with the carriage shed just to the left of the signal. The men are posing on an engine that was built in Wolverhampton in 1869 and was bought by the Bishop's Castle Railway in 1905.

There were two general and agricultural ironmongers in Bishop's Castle. They were Arthur Greenhous, who traded from 7 Market Square, and Edward Davies, whose shop was at 34 and 36 High Street. He succeeded Robert Norton and Son, who had been dealing in the town for several generations. Before moving to these premises they had a shop in Church Street where they also sold wines and spirits. In 1896 they were advertised as, 'General and furnishing ironmongers, tinmen, braziers, seedsmen, agents for agricultural implements and dairy appliances.' Standing in the doorway are Mr Edward Davies and his son Charles, who later inherited the business.

This is a view of the Bishop's Castle Railway near Plowden Station on 14 May 1936, the year after the line was closed. The train being pulled by the engine *Carlisle* is the demolition or dismantling train used to tear up the line and recover the sleepers. The *Carlisle* was the favourite engine on the Bishop's Castle line and was bought by the company in 1895. It was a six-coupled engine with a four wheeled tender and was built in 1868 by Kidsons of Leeds. While at Bishop's Castle the tender was fitted with a weatherboard to protect the driver and fireman from the elements when running tender first. The hills in the background are part of the Long Mynd.

Plowden Station was the second station on the Bishop's Castle Railway. Trains bound for Bishop's Castle would depart from the north bay at Craven Arms, heading towards Shrewsbury on the main line for about a mile, before turning off at Stretford Bridge Junction. A short halt was erected there and the train would stop if required. The train then ran along a single track until it reached Horderley Station, which had its platform on one side of the line and the station buildings on the other! Between Horderley and Plowden the train crossed the river Onny three times and passed through more beautiful scenery. After leaving Plowden the train went into a wooded cutting and the Onny was crossed again on several occasions before Lydham Heath Station was reached. At Lydham Heath the engine was attached to the other end of the train and, after entering a spur, set off on its final leg to Bishop's Castle. The station at Lytham was small and built out of wood but Plowden, which was the largest on the line, was constructed out of red brick like Eaton and Horderley.

This aerial view of Craven Arms and Stokesay railway station is looking north towards Shrewsbury. The main station and platforms are on the right. The buildings to the left of the station are the engine sheds, while those in the top right-hand corner are the carriage sheds. The buildings and the piles of tree trunks in the centre belong to J.C. Edge &Co. Ltd. The firm, which later became known as Bendware, opened their timber business there in 1912. Bendware made a variety of sporting goods, including tennis and badminton rackets, cricket bats and billiard cues. The site was developed into housing in the 1980s. The road leading away from the signal box is Brook Street.

This photograph was taken by R.N. Haywood in about 1915 and shows postman Fred Mole making one of his daily visits to empty a most unusual letterbox that was situated inside the trunk of the Old Oak, about a mile and a half from Clun near the top of the Oak Bank. Postman Mole was based at Clun, where the postmistress was Mrs Jessie Lewis. Part of his duty was to drive the post cart twice a day between Clun and Aston-on-Clun to fetch and carry mail and to empty post boxes between the two places. The hollow inside the tree was big enough to accommodate several people and at first the post office thought that it was ideal for a box. Unfortunately the oak often gave shelter to gypsies and vagrants and was beginning to cause traffic problems as it took up half the road. Both the tree and the box were removed in the 1930s.

The Clun Valley Motor Service belonged to the Ludlow Motor Garage, which had depots in Ludlow and Craven Arms. It is parked outside the post office in the Square at Clun. The service ran from Clun to Craven Arms Station twice a day in 1917, at 9.30am and 5pm, and returned at 11.15am and 7pm. The driver of this bus is Bert Wood and two of his passengers are Thomas Davies, the baker wearing the trilby, and behind him Alfred Stringer, the landlord of the Buffalo Hotel. Another driver was Harry Peplow, who was also the landlord of the Tile Tavern. His vehicle was known as 'Pep's Bus' and he is remembered for his accuracy in delivering papers from his moving bus onto the doorsteps of the cottages as he passed. More unkindly, one driver was known as 'Conk' because of his large nose and his bus was known as 'Conk's Henhouse'.

Most of the old buildings in Aston-on-Clun are built out of stone, including two unusual round houses. They were built by a rather eccentric inhabitant in about 1800 with this one, just above the Kangaroo Inn, said to be the better preserved. Between the round house and the Kangaroo Inn was the village blacksmith's shop. The smithy was run for many years by the Jones family, who were successful in adapting the business from horse drawn transport to motorized, calling their old blacksmith's shop Forge Garage. The men standing outside the forge are probably William Jones and his son.

This is a rare view of the old railway station at Church Stretton that stood to the north of the bridge and the present station. The engine is travelling towards Craven Arms and Hereford. This station, with its main building and canopy on the left, was built by the Shrewsbury to Hereford Railway in 1852. The main platforms were 170ft long, with a cattle bay measuring 200ft. The structure behind the first telegraph pole on the left is the water column and coal office. Just beyond the water column are cattle pens and a crane. The line going off to the left led to the goods shed and the two wagon turntables. The signal box is on the right above the platform and the lady with the umbrella is standing outside a small waiting room. Melrose and Buchanan's whiskies are advertised on the station as well as Sutton's Seeds. Today the station building is a private house.

Mr and Mrs John Lewis stand outside their stationery shop and post office in Clungunford. The Lewis family had lived in the village for a number of years and before taking over the post office both Mr Lewis and his father were the local saddlers and harness makers. In 1885 the mail was still being delivered from Aston-on-Clun, the nearest post office, but by 1895 a village post office was opened by William Jones, who was also registered as a castrator! John Lewis became sub-postmaster in about 1905 and he was succeeded by his daughter Mary. Note the two heavy sacks for the postman to deliver by Mrs Lewis' feet.

On 23 May 1914 a new station was opened at Church Stretton to the south of the bridge. This view is looking towards Shrewsbury with the arch of the bridge clearly visible. The new station was built to cope with the growing amount of traffic and longer trains, with the platforms being extended to 551ft in length. The main station building is on the left, but there were two waiting rooms on both sides with fine glazed canopies. A covered footbridge linked the platforms. Goods traffic used the station until September 1966 and the following year the station was left unmanned. In February 1970 the station was extensively modernised, leading to the destruction of a great deal of GWR-designed architecture.

Beambridge is situated half a mile up the valley from Munslow on the road to Much Wenlock. Apart from a few isolated buildings there is nothing there apart from the smithy, which is a 19th-century folly, the front being built in the Gothic style with a castellated top, which is hidden by ivy in this view. In 1885 the blacksmith was Thomas Wall. Twenty years later his wife Mary was running the business. Note the three blacksmiths working on the plough and the weather vane protruding through the ivy. The man on the right is Fred Freeman and the man on the left is his son, who is also called Fred. They were known locally as 'Owd Fred' and 'Young Fred' and were running the forge by 1917. The young man in the middle is Charles Edwards, the apprentice blacksmith. He opened his own forge at Bache Mill, Diddlebury. He later became farrier to William Hyde at Laughton Stables and worked at race meetings throughout the country.

John Joseph Lakelin, perhaps the man at the gate, was the sub-postmaster of Longden for over 40 years. He was first listed in the village in 1891 as the sub-postmaster with letters arriving from Shrewsbury at 8am and returning at 5.10pm. The nearest money order office was at Hanwood and the telegraph office was at Hanwood railway station. By 1900 Mr Lakelin was also the village baker and confectioner, a function he continued until about 1920, before leaving the appropriately named Mr Sidney Bunn of Annscroft as the only baker in the area. The post office is now situated in a single-storey building attached to the left-hand side of the old post office.

The old bridge at Minsterley was judged to be unsafe and it was replaced in 1909. The replacement is a portal framed bridge, where the deck is rigidly attached to the abutments, giving it great strength. A.T. Davies, the County Surveyor, designed the bridge and also supervised the construction. Before the bridge was opened on 14 January 1910 it was tested for strength by two large traction engines with a combined weight of over 28 tons. Note the men beneath the bridge, monitoring the structure for movement; apparently it moved just $1/30$ of an inch. The bridge has a span of 30 feet and was constructed by the Liverpool-based Hennebique Ferro-Concrete Contracting Company at a cost of around £396.

The new bridge in Minsterley spans a fast flowing tributary of the Rea Brook. The opening of the bridge and the arrival of the two steam engines caused quite a stir and officials share the moment with a group of boys and men from the village. The man with the beard on the left wearing a cassock and cape is the Revd R.W. Williams, who was vicar of the parish for about 40 years. On the extreme right is Thomas Hutton, who lived at Minsterley Hall. He was a land and estate agent, surveyor and valuer and agent to the Marquess of Bath.

The railway line between Shrewsbury and Minsterley was opened on 14 February 1861. The line was nine and a half miles in length and had stations at Hanwood, Plealey Road and Pontesbury. The station at Minsterley had a number of useful facilities including a milk wharf, goods shed, cattle and horse docks and a number of sidings. Passenger traffic was stopped in 1951 and freight traffic by 1967; the track was lifted in 1973. The steam saw mill was owned by Robert Price, a builder and timber merchant, who also traded as a coal, lime and corn dealer. In 1895 he advertised that Dutch barn erecting was a speciality of his firm and his prices were low irrespective of the distance. He sold the business as a going concern in October 1898 before embarking on a new venture by opening a large dairy and creamery in the village.

Until the middle of the last century it was not unusual to see a number of tradesmen like milk roundsmen and postmen working on Christmas Day. Here we see postal staff ready to deliver the mail to the villages and hamlets around Minsterley. The building behind used to be a post office and was located on the road from Minsterley to Horsebridge. The man on the left with the beard is Thomas Williams, whose round stretched from Minsterley to the Bog on the top of the Stiperstones. He carried out his duties for 33 years, without ever having a holiday, with no time off for ill-health and even working on Christmas Day. During his career as a postman it was estimated that he had walked over 165,000 miles.

In some areas of Shropshire at the close of the 19th century life could still be very harsh, especially for those entering or leaving the world. There was no National Health Service and medical treatment was expensive and in places like the Stiperstones could be a long time arriving. In such communities there was always someone people could turn to in times of trouble. Such a lady was Mrs Hannah Perkins, who lived at Perkins Beach near the Stiperstones. She acted as the local midwife in the area and was always on hand to help the dying and to prepare them properly for burial after their death. Although she died herself in the 1920s she is well remembered and very well thought of.

Lead mining has taken place in the Snailbeach area since Roman times, but began in earnest in the 17th century. It was by far the richest lead mine in Shropshire, producing over 131,000 tons of lead ore between 1845 and 1913 when it closed. The photographer is looking west over a great deal of industrial activity in about 1900. Bottom left is the Snailbeach Narrow Gauge Railway. Just 2ft 4in inches wide and around three miles long, it was opened in 1877 and connected the mine to the Pontesbury sidings. The line can also be seen on the right between the white building and Black Tom Shaft winding gear; the shaft was sunk in 1820. The building with the two gable ends in the centre is the loco shed and to the left of that are the new crusher and compressor houses.

This view was taken from near Lord's Hill looking down the valley over the Snailbeach mine reservoir. The reservoir was built in 1872 and was used to overcome water shortages during a period of drought. The pumping house on the hill to the left usually brought water up to drainage level before emptying it into Hope Brook almost a mile away, but in drought conditions it was capable of raising water to the surface. The railway track in the foreground was used to move lead ore from Lords Hill Mine.

Chirbury lies close to the Welsh border just two miles from Offa's Dyke in a valley with views across to the high crests of the Berwyns. Standing outside his grocery and bakery shop on Salop Road is William Pritchard with his wife and perhaps his two sons; across the road is his delivery cart complete with baskets of bread. Later Mr Pritchard went into business with a Mr Green and they took over the shop and post office in Broad Street. The shop has been demolished but the cottages on the right are still standing. Note the prettily dressed girls standing smartly by the pavement perhaps with their mother or their teacher. The village hall that was built in 1912 now occupies the site behind them.

A steam engine is photographed together with some of the inhabitants on the main road through Marton, which lies close to the Welsh border 15 miles south-west of Shrewsbury. There are three other villages called Marton in Shropshire. One is near Baschurch and Old Marton and New Marton are near Ellesmere. The name is derived from 'the settlement by the mere' and refers to Marton Pool, which lies just to the east of the village. At one time the pool covered over 30 acres but it has been reduced in size over the years, although it is still large enough for sailing. The girls are standing in the garden of the village shop, which was occupied by the Misses Oliver. They ran the post office from these premises and sold a variety of groceries and clothing.

Two railway staff and one passenger wait for the Central Wales train to Swansea to stop at Dorrington Station in the 1930s. Dorrington was the second station after Condover on the line out of Shrewsbury. The line opened in 1849 and became jointly owned by the Great Western and the London North West Railway companies in 1854. The line is still open but smaller stations like Condover and Dorrington were closed to passengers on 9 June 1958 and to goods traffic on 15 March 1965. In 1853 it took around two and a half hours to travel from Shrewsbury to Hereford, stopping at all the smaller stations. The fare from Shrewsbury to Dorrington was 1s 6d first class, 1 shilling second class, 9d third class and 6d Parliamentary class, which allowed the poor to travel sitting on old wooden benches. The engine pulling the train is an LMS locomotive known as a 'Black Five'. Note the milk churns on both platforms waiting to be picked up. The station had its own dairy on site and each day a milk train known as 'The Dorrington to Kensington Milk' ran from the village to the capital.

The blacksmith's shop in Dorrington was a very important establishment in the village for hundreds of years. From the middle of the 19th century several generations of the Glover family ran the business after they took it over from William Pugh. As well as shoeing horses, they were also able to make and repair a wide variety of farm machinery. It seems the Glovers also looked after the feet of humans, as the signs over the main door are advertising reliable shoes and boots and Bradley's boot polish. The building in the background is the village hall.

The posters on the wall date this photograph to early 1909, when John Bevan was the village blacksmith in Longnor. He was there from around 1890 until 1913 when the business was obtained by Richard Higgs, a local farmer. The bottom poster is advertising the Great Horse Fair held at the Raven Repository in Shrewsbury on Tuesday 2 March by auctioneers Hall, Wateridge and Owen. The poster above, which is slightly hidden by the open half door, is advertising another sale by Jackson and McCartney of Craven Arms of 17 cattle, 121 sheep, four horses and a quantity of household furniture. The large poster on the left is advertising the shop, in Mardol Head, Shrewsbury, of John Kent, a silversmith and jeweller.

The staff pose for the photographer in this very rare view of Leebotwood railway station. The station was erected in 1853, the year after the Shrewsbury to Hereford line was opened to traffic. It once employed a stationmaster, two assistants and four men to work in shifts in the signal box. A great deal of local produce was sent out by rail and local farmers also had animal feed and livestock delivered from market. Next to the station was a coal wharf, which was once run by the Everson family, who also supplied building material to the area and were the licensees of the Pound Inn. The man in the doorway looks like the stationmaster, who in 1900 was Thomas J. Perks. The station closed in 1958.

Stone has been quarried from the side of Pontesbury Hill since 1827. In 1900 the quarries were owned by Richard Pugh and William Toye, a coal factor, builders' merchant and a former mayor of Shrewsbury. He advertised in 1905: 'Stone in various sizes for road making, as used by the Railway Companies, County and District Councils; also chippings for Garden Walks and Drives, supplied in Truck Loads from our own Quarries'. By the 1930s the quarries were owned by Basil Timmis and S.J. Haywood & Co. Mr Haywood owned the Nills Hill Quarry, which he first leased to the County Council and finally sold to it in 1954. The quarry was a magnet for children, who enjoyed playing a variety of games there after the workers had gone home. Some got up to mischief, annoying the nightwatchman by placing clods of turf over the chimney of his hut and smoking him out. This quarry was known locally as the Rock but its official name was Nills Hill Quarry.

This view of Pontesbury and Nills Hill Quarry was taken from Pontesbury Hill. The entrance to the quarry was at the top of a steep bank near the Weaver's Cottages. The building in the bottom left-hand corner is the tarmac-loading bay; the building with the wheel is the stone crushing plant, which is hiding the stone-loading bay in front of it. Note the kerbing stones piled to the right of the buildings. People who lived in cottages nearby remember the siren sounding twice a day to warn of the imminent explosion that would shake their homes.

The blacksmith's shop was situated in Castle Pulverbatch and from 1890 until the 1940s it was operated by the Griffith family, first by Edwin Griffith and then by his son Frederick. Note the blacksmith on the right. Tales of witchcraft were common in the Pulverbatch area. One old woman called Betty Chidley used to go round the village begging for things that took her fancy. At one farm she saw some food being mixed for the calves and took a fancy to it, but was told she could not have any. Betty told the farmer's wife in a menacing voice, 'the calves wunna eat the suppin' now' and as much as they tried the animals would not go near it. Betty was asked back to the farm and after being pacified by the farmer's wife said 'God bless the calves' and to the owner's delight the hungry animals were waiting eagerly for their dinner.

This view of Craven Arms and Stokesay railway station was taken in about 1910. The platforms are almost deserted, an unusual sight for a normally busy station, where the occasional accident has occurred. On a foggy evening in September 1913 a fruit train from Hereford had just pulled into the station when a passenger train from Central Wales came around the curve. Fortunately the passenger train had slowed down but the engine still crashed into the back of the fruit train, smashing the buffers on the guard's van and shaking the passengers. The only casualty was the guard of the fruit train who sustained a broken arm. After first aid had been administered in the waiting room he was transported back to Hereford on the Bristol Express.

Chapter Four
Hotels, Inns and Hostelries

This house in Ludford, known as the Old Bell, was built in the early 17th century for Humphrey Powell, a member of the Council of the Marches. It became an inn from an early date and was first known as the Three Crowns and then the Bell. In the 18th century it was a coaching house on the busy road into Herefordshire but when a new road bypassed it in the 1820s it was converted into a pair of cottages and the name was transferred to another inn at the bottom of Broad Street. In 1910 the house was converted back to a single dwelling.

This view of the Salway Arms at Wooferton was taken in around 1921 when the proprietor was Albert Moulton. The inn was given a full licence in 1853. In 1900 the owner was Mrs O'Brien of Moor Park, Ludlow, and the landlady was Elizabeth Susannah Gittins. Accommodation at that time consisted of a bar, three parlours, a kitchen and eight bedrooms. There was also room in the stables for eight horses. The inn was reported to be in good repair and clean and it did most of its trade with agricultural workers and passing travellers. Being situated two miles from the nearest police station may have led to the following prosecutions. The first was on 13 June 1881, when the landlord was found guilty of selling alcohol to a drunken person and was fined £2 plus 16 shillings costs. On New Year's Eve 1894 Mrs Gittins was found guilty of keeping her house open for the consumption of alcohol during prohibited hours; she was fined 10 shillings with costs of 6 shillings.

Standing in a most picturesque position at one end of the Ludford Bridge on the banks of the River Teme is the Charlton Arms. It has been known by this name since the 19th century, when it was granted a licence by magistrates in Leominster in 1846. It is named after the Charlton family who owned land in the area but before that it was known as the Red Lion. Around 1900 the inn belonged to John Gilbert and W.A. Smith, who ran the Lichfield Brewery, and it could sell only their beer. Its accommodation consisted of a bar, parlour, smokeroom, kitchen and eight bedrooms, all of which were considered to be in good repair and clean. There was also enough stabling at the rear for 15 horses. The customers were described as agricultural workers and people passing the inn. As the 20th century progressed the inn tried to broaden its appeal by building a dance hall and providing lawns for Clock Golf, but both have disappeared under the car park. By the 1950s the pub was advertised as a free house selling Ansells and Worthington and other popular beers. They catered for both large and small parties, serving afternoon teas in the garden and evening meals and grills in the dining room.

The Broad Gate even in the early days of motoring was not built for the motor car. The gateway's two semi-circular towers of stone are late mediaeval, and the portcullis grooves and gate hinges date from the 14th century. The western drum tower has been hidden by a Regency extension and mock battlements were added in the 18th century. The Wheatsheaf on the right is built in the town ditch and was first recorded in 1753. It is reputed to be the last public house in Ludlow to brew its own beer. In 1900 the owner and landlord was Henry Rogers and the premises consisted of a bar, parlour, kitchen and five bedrooms. There was stabling for three horses and the house and stables were said to be clean and in a good state of repair. John Langley, a coal merchant from 25 Corve Street, has left his horse and dray outside the inn, perhaps to enjoy a well-earned pint after a long day's work.

The Angel Hotel in Broad Street, Ludlow, with its two 18th-century bow windows, has been an inn since 1551. It was one of the town's principal coaching inns, with its most famous coach, the *Aurora*, making the trip between Ludlow and London in just 24 hours in the 1820s. Horatio Nelson was given the Freedom of the Borough in 1802 while he was staying at the hotel with his mistress Emma and her husband Sir William Hamilton. The room where the honour was presented to him was later known as the Nelson Room. When they arrived in the town a cheering crowd pulled their coach through the streets. Nelson thanked the citizens of Ludlow for the honour by addressing a large crowd from one of the bay windows. Napoleon's brother Lucien Bonaparte is reputed to have dined there while a prisoner of war in the town in 1814. During World War Two the army requisitioned it and part of it was converted into a British Restaurant, one of the self-service establishments that sprang up during this period. Towards the end of the 20th century the hotel closed and has been converted into a number of retail shops.

The Ludlow Arms stood on the Whitcliffe Road in an old timber-framed building. The inn had a fine bowling green and has been known at different times as the Whitcliffe or Bowling Green Inn. In 1900 it was owned by Lord Windsor of Oakley Park and the landlord was Henry Crane. The inn was described as clean and in good repair and consisted of a bar, billiards room, kitchen and three bedrooms, with stables for four horses. In 1901 it was reported that the stables need repairing and whitewashing. About 1960 the inn was owned by Davenports, who advertised: 'For centuries this ancient inn has extended a warmth of greeting and a standard of hospitality which has made it famous amongst famous inns and a calling place of travellers from far and near. Today the Ludlow Arms has lost none of its ancient loveliness, yet everything has been done to add to its comforts. It is the perfect blending of old-world charm with the advantages of the present.' The Bowling Green closed in 1968 and was converted into a private hotel and later into a house.

In 1891 the Feathers Hotel in Ludlow was advertised as 'One of the oldest established commercial houses in the kingdom'. It was also a posting house and the proprietor Charles Edwards was able to furnish customers with carriages for weddings and transport for funerals in a new funeral hearse with glass or panelled sides. He hired out a variety of vehicles that included flies, broughams, brakes and private omnibuses and also post or saddle horses, all let at the shortest notice and at very reasonable terms. By 1900 the hotel was owned by Mrs Jane Edwards of Lee Cottage, Torrington Park, North Finchley, London, but leased to the Church Stretton Hotel Company. Accommodation at the hotel included a bar, bar parlour, two smoke rooms, a market room, a commercial room, a coffee room, a billiard room, sitting, drawing and dining rooms and 21 bedrooms. The landlady was Mrs Harriet A. Beard.

The first stone of the Temperance Coffee House and Reading Room in Craven Arms was laid in May 1865 by Miss Lumb, the daughter of the Revd W.E. Lumb, vicar of Halford. It was later renamed the Temperance Hotel and by 1885 was advertised as a 'Family and Commercial Hotel adjoining the railway station; good accommodation for commercial gentlemen, every comfort for tourists, good fishing, horses and traps for hire, terms moderate'. During World War Two the army requisitioned it and did not hand it back until March 1951. At first it was hoped to convert the building into housing, but this was rejected as too costly. The building was sold to a private owner in 1965 and in the year 2005 there are rumours that the building, which has been labelled 'an eyesore', may be demolished and the site used for housing.

Purslow stands on the B4368 midway between Aston-on-Clun and Clunton. The Hundred House is a substantial building that was first recorded as a hostelry in the middle of the 18th century. In 1901 the inn belonged to the Earl of Powis. Edward Smith was landlord for a number of years and was considered a good manager, providing a first-class service for his customers. However, he did find himself in trouble with the law in January 1888, when he was fined 10 shillings plus 7 shillings costs for keeping the inn open during prohibited hours. The sign over the left window informed customers that the Hundred House was fully licensed and provided luncheons, dinners, teas and good stabling; while the one on the right tells them that the inn is under the management of the People's Refreshment House Association Ltd. Throughout the 19th century a two-day hare coursing event was held at Purslow, which was supported mainly by farmers and local people from the Bishop's Castle and Clun area. The event, which was last recorded in 1890, always ended with a dinner at the Hundred House. Until about 1880 Purslow Races also combined athletic competitions between men and horses.

As you crossed the Bottom Bridge in Bucknell and entered the Square the Plough Inn was situated on the left-hand side. At the beginning of the 20th century the inn was owned by a Miss Stedman, who lived at New House in the village. The Dodd family managed the inn but by 1905 it had been taken over by the Morris family. Both families were blacksmiths and to supplement their income they ran the village forge at the left of the inn. An 1896 census informs us that the inn was considered to have good accommodation and stabling for six horses. Most of its custom came from agricultural workers and passing trade.

The Black Lion stood on the corner of Welsh Street and Union Street in Bishop's Castle and was built in the 17th century. It was first recorded as a pub in about 1792 and by 1900 it was owned by Lassell and Sharman's Brewery, which was based in Flintshire. It was one of nearly 30 public houses in the town but today it is a private house. In 1900 the landlord was John Grovenor. He was said to be a good manager and kept the house in good repair. The customers at this time were farmers and agricultural workers and people who frequented the market. There was also stabling for 12 horses at the rear. The photograph was taken in about 1920, when the landlord was Allan Davies.

The Bull Inn stood in Bull Street, Bishop's Castle, and was first licensed in about 1792. The inn was owned by John Henry Carless of Barrow-in-Furness, who leased it to the Shrewsbury brewer Thomas Southam. The landlord in 1901 was Edward Mansell, who was reported to be a good manager, keeping his house clean and in good repair. His customers were described as agricultural workers and people frequenting the Market Hall that can be seen just below the inn. On 7 September 1897 Mr Mansell had trouble with the law when he was taken to court and fined £1 plus 15 shillings costs for permitting drunkenness on his licensed premises. Presumably the people standing at the door are members of the Reece family, who were living at the inn for a short period at the end of the 19th century.

The Castle Hotel was built in around 1720 on the site of the outer bailey of the bishop's castle that gave the town its name. By this time very little of the original structure was left, but a great deal of the rubble that remained was used as hardcore for the bowling green. In the survey of public houses in 1901 it was reported that the owner of the hotel was Lord Powis and the landlord was Thomas George. Accommodation at the house was considered good, although some repairs were being carried out to the building. The customers were classed as commercial and agricultural workers and there was good stabling with room for 30 horses.

The Buffalo Hotel stands in the Square in Clun and has been an inn since the 18th century. In about 1900 it was owned by the Ludlow and Craven Arms Brewery and the landlord was Arthur King. On the back of the card, written in 1931 by the father of Mrs J. Hall of Belle Vue Gardens, Shrewsbury, is the message: 'I stayed here last night, quite a good and reasonable inn. It is the inn Sir Walter Scott stayed at and I slept in the same room he slept in and they did not charge any extra.' Sir Walter Scott spent several weeks at the hotel in the 1820s while writing the novel *The Betrothed*, which he reputedly set around Clun Castle.

The Royal George stood on the corner of High Street and Ford Street in Clun. It was named after an 18th-century man-of-war and was known locally as the Ship. At the beginning of the 19th century it was occupied by John Hints and run as a temperance hotel. It had closed by the 1930s and was converted into refreshment and tearooms by Miss Nellie Hints. There was another temperance hotel in the High Street, known as the Jubilee Commercial House, which was run by Edward Vaughn. In 1896 the hotel advertised 'Delightful Situation, Splendid Scenery, Home Comforts. Every Accommodation for Families and Commercial Travellers. Excellent Trout Fishing Near The Town'. This hotel had also closed by the 1930s. The building at the rear of the Royal George is the Primitive Methodist Chapel.

The Rocke Arms at Abcot was situated just across the river from Clungunford, not far from the church, which can be seen through the trees. It was a free house and in 1901 it belonged to J.C.S. Rocke from Clungunford, whose family it was named after. It was occupied at this time by William Bowen, who was considered a good manager and kept a clean and tidy house. The inn catered for agricultural workers and travellers and was still open in 1917, but by 1921 it had closed and was occupied by Miss Maud Herbert, who rented out rooms in the house. Perhaps the little boy by the front door with the dog is one of Mr Bowen's children.

The Crown Inn at Newcastle-on-Clun received its first licence at the beginning of the 19th century. It was owner occupied and in 1901 the landlord was Richard Jones, who also ran the village shop. The accommodation at the inn was considered to be fairly good but the house did need some repair. Note the little girl standing on the mounting block, put there for the benefit of customers too drunk to mount their horses in the conventional way after a good night out. There was also a boarding house in the village, which was run by the Richardsons. Mrs Richardson was well remembered for her large dinners and walkers were advised to do at least a 16-mile hike after breakfast before tackling one of her meals. Her husband was also considered 'a hearty chap as any with whom you have swapped yarns and paid turns about the village alehouse'.

The building in the centre is Church Stretton's town hall and market, which was situated in the High Street. The traders sold their wares beneath the arches, while the business of the town was conducted in the room above. The upper storey was also used for concerts and public meetings and had a capacity of around 250. In 1869 fortnightly penny readings took place there for the benefit of the working classes. Three inns surrounded the hall; to the left was the Raven, to the right the Plough, and almost opposite the Lion. The Raven had been a public house since the 18th century and occupied buildings once belonging to the Bright family of Little Stretton. In 1896 it belonged to W.J. Roberts of Newport, but by 1901 he had sold it to T. Cooper's Brewery at Burton-on-Trent. The Lion was owned by Robert McCartney in 1896 but was managed by George Marsh. The inn was also known as the Red Lion and after it closed it became a haberdashery shop and then a newsagents.

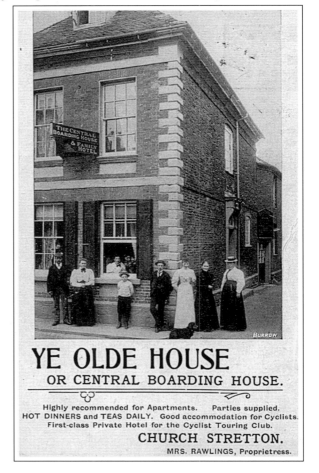

This photograph of the Central Hotel in Church Stretton was taken from a publicity postcard, which calls the establishment Ye Olde House. The building was erected in a narrow opening at the beginning of the 18th century and is a fine example of a Queen Anne house. In 1898 Henry Rawlings bought it for £1,000 and his wife Frances ran it as a boarding house and family hotel. In 1910 a very busy Mrs Rawlings writes to her mother-in-law, who was staying at Dursley in Gloucestershire: 'Thank you for your letter. All well. Full up, 20. You can tell I have not much spare time. With Love Frances'.

The Denehurst Hotel was built on the Shrewsbury Road at Church Stretton at the end of the 19th century. It was a private house occupied by a Mrs Jones until about 1914. By 1917 it had been converted into a boarding house run by Leonard Jones, and by 1928 it was advertised as a private hotel under the management of Mr and Mrs Barron. The hotel was always popular and in recent times hosted cabaret dinners where many top stars performed. In about 1990 a leisure centre was opened with a swimming pool, sauna, jacuzzi, gymnasium and solarium. The hotel was demolished in 2001 and a splendid new housing complex for senior citizens has been built on the site.

The Long Mynd Hotel at Church Stretton was erected in 1899 as the town was beginning to grow into a holiday and retirement spa. It was built for the Church Stretton Hydropathic Syndicate and for the first years of its life was called the Hydro Hotel. It was advertised in 1900 as a first-class family and residential hotel set in 12 acres of beautifully wooded grounds. Its facilities included many spa treatments including Turkish, medical and other baths. You could also participate in billiards, tennis, croquet and golf, or you could go hunting with four packs of hounds. When first built, the hotel had a pitched roof with dormer windows. Some years later a flat roof replaced the old one after two extra floors were added. Perhaps E. C. Harris, who wrote this postcard to Miss G. Bennett of Leyton, was involved with this work. He wrote: 'Dear Miss B. Have been working out here for a few days. Am staying at this hotel which we are engaged in altering.'

The Hotel in Church Stretton was sited on the corner of Sandford Avenue and Shrewsbury Road. It was built in three phases on the site of a farmhouse, an inn and a malt house. The first phase on the corner in 1861 replaced the Crown Inn and malt house. The second phase on Sandford Avenue was built in 1899, and the final phase along the Shrewsbury Road, on the site of the farmhouse, was completed in 1906. To the right of the second large window from the steps an inscribed stone from the old malt house has been retained. It reads: 'erected by Copper A W his sonne Ano Dni 1587'. In April 1962 five people perished as a dreadful fire gutted the hotel. The building has since been broken down into smaller units, which include flats, shops and a public house.

At the beginning of the 20th century Mrs Harriet Hardy ran the Sandford House Boarding Establishment in Church Stretton. At that time the tariff was 5s 6d or 8 shillings per day according to the season. The establishment also had links with the Stretton Boarding House by the North Pier in Blackpool. By 1921 her son Charles had upgraded it to a private hotel. During the 1930s it was described as 'Conveniently Situated and AA Appointed'. It was an unlicensed premises until January 1948, when the Plough Inn closed in the High Street and its licence transferred to the Sandford. The hotel closed in the 1980s and was converted into a nursing home.

The Ragleth Inn was one of three public houses listed in Little Stretton in the early years of the 20th century. The inn was known as the Sun until about 1907, when it changed its name to commemorate a local hill. In 1901 William Speake, who lived in the village and was listed as a farmer, owned the Sun Inn. He rented it to Edward Lewis, who was a good manager and kept the house 'clean and in fair repair'. A previous landlord was not so particular and he was taken to court for allowing drunkenness in his house on Christmas Day in 1887. He was fined £5 plus 12s 2d costs. By the 1930s the hostelry was offering visitors luncheons, teas, bed and breakfast or full board, as well as providing all the usual services of a village inn.

Riders call for refreshments at the Swan Inn, Aston Munslow, as horsemen have been doing for at least 200 years. The old timber-framed house was given its first full licence in about 1790. In 1896 the Trustees of Ludlow Municipal Charities owned the hostelry but by 1901 they had sold it to the Ludlow and Craven Arms Brewery. Joseph Cooper was landlord in 1896 when the accommodation consisted of a kitchen, two parlours, a bar, five bedrooms and stabling for five horses. The house was said to be in a fair condition but needed cleaning. Five years later the condition of the inn had not improved and it was stated, 'the house requires papering and painting throughout and the stables are out of repair'. The report also reveals that although the inn was two miles from the nearest constable station they were caught by the law for 'permitting drunkenness', and were fined £2 plus 13s 8d costs. There is also a claim that the famous highwayman Dick Turpin lodged at the inn.

Landlord Henry Marsh poses with some of his customers outside his inn, the Royal Oak in Cardington. He was landlord of the Royal Oak from about 1895 until the mid-1930s. He was well known around the village as he was also the local boot maker, assistant overseer and rate collector. The owner of the Royal Oak in 1901 was Henry Reddin, a grocer, boot maker and wine and spirit merchant from Church Stretton. Mr Marsh was considered a good manager who kept his inn clean and in good repair. He was also very law-abiding and had no convictions, perhaps because a constable was stationed in the village. There was stabling for seven horses behind the inn and the bulk of his customers were agricultural workers and passing trade. Note the Royal Insurance fire plaque to the left of the inn sign.

The Sun Inn at Corfton has been serving beer since at least 1770 when it was granted its first full licence. In 1901 Edward Wood JP, of Culmington Hall, owned the Sun. Edwin Cox was landlord and he had taken over from his father William. Accommodation at the house in 1901 consisted of a kitchen, a bar, two parlours and seven bedrooms. Edwin was considered a good host who kept his house clean and in good repair. The inn was later occupied by Sidney Cadwallader, who in the 1930s saw the full potential of the motor car and opened up a garage on both sides of the road by his inn. The signs show that the inn was a free house selling Bass and Butler's ales, and that the garage stocked Castrol oil, Good Year tyres, Exide batteries and Shell petrol at 1s 5d a gallon.

The Bath Arms stood on Station Road in Minsterley until it was demolished for housing in 2004. It was named after the Marquess of Bath, who was the proprietor and one of the principal landowners in the area. The Lee family, who were also listed as farmers, ran it for over 60 years between 1870 and 1935. Accommodation in 1901 consisted of two kitchens, a bar, two parlours, a clubroom, five bedrooms and a cellar. Around 1920 landlord John Lee went into partnership with a relative, possibly his brother, and opened a garage next door. Note the sign on the side of the inn. They were advertised as 'automobile, electrical, motor and general engineers'. They also had cars for hire. A small estate of houses called Bath Mews now occupies the site.

Situated at the top of Salop Street in Bishop's Castle is the Castle Hotel. On the left is the Three Tuns Inn and Brewery. The inn dates back to at least 1642, the year it was granted its first full licence. In 1888 John Roberts, a London tea taster, who wanted to escape the unhealthy climate of the capital, bought the Three Tuns. He set up a new brewery and employed his cousin, who was a teetotaller, as head brewer. The Roberts family were connected with the inn for three generations until John and Gwen Roberts retired in 1976.

This is a view of Crowsnest Dingle from the side of Oak Hill, looking back towards Snailbeach. The Cross Guns Inn occupied the building on the right from about 1838 until the early 1930s. In 1901 the inn belonged to the Marquess of Bath, one of the big landowners in the area. The accommodation at this time consisted of a kitchen, a bar, a parlour, two bedrooms, a back kitchen and a cellar. At the rear of the building was a clubhouse, which had a billiard table, where dances were held and dance lessons given. The last landlord of the inn was William John Salter. Dingle is the local name for a valley.

The Herbert Arms at Chirbury was named in honour of Lord Herbert, who was created first Lord of Chirbury in 1629. He was said to be a man of 'wide learning, great wit and undoubted valour'. After his death he left a valuable collection of chained books in the old School House, which is now preserved in the county's archives. The inn is very large and in 1896 it belonged to Lord Powis of Powis Castle, Welshpool. The landlord was Thomas White, who was considered an able manager. The inn was frequented by local farmers and agricultural workers and also commercial travellers and tourists. The house was clean and in good repair and the accommodation consisted of two kitchens, a bar parlour, a parlour, two sitting rooms, a clubroom, cellars and 14 bedrooms.

Today the main road through Marton is very busy, but the Sun Inn is still open to cater for the needs of passing travellers and also as a social venue for the village. In 1862 the Sun was sold to John Medlicott, who owned land around the inn, for £756 10s 0d. It was described as a profitable business, being in the middle of the village on the turnpike road from Shrewsbury to Montgomery. The inn is built out of stone and in 1896 was occupied by Elizabeth Carryer. The owner was D. Dawson, a brewer from Newtown, but by 1901 he had sold it to Lassell and Sharman of the Wrexham Brewery Company. In 1896 accommodation at the Sun consisted of a bar, a bar parlour, a parlour, a sitting room, a kitchen and back kitchen, five bedrooms and a cellar. For trade the landlady relied upon local agricultural workers and travellers.

The main road passes through Dorrington on its way towards Shrewsbury. The post office and the Horseshoes Inn are on the left. For many years the Horseshoes was a free house and was able to brew its own beer. The car in the distance has just passed a house dated 1846, which stands on the corner of Lower Fold and was once the home of William Morris, a harness maker. The village's most famous son is John Boydell, an engraver and publisher, who was born in Dorrington in 1719 and became Lord Mayor of London in 1790.

Leebotwood takes its name from the clearing in the forest of Botwood. This photograph, looking south towards Church Stretton, was taken in about 1900 when Thomas Hotchkiss Everson was landlord of the Pound Inn. The owner of the inn was the Revd F.H.W. Whitmore of Dudmaston, who had sold it to the People's Refreshment House Association by 1917. In 1901 the inn consisted of a bar, a parlour, a private room, a kitchen, three cellars and four bedrooms. The house also contains some fine oak panelling, which is thought to originate from Woolstaston Rectory. The inn takes its name from the enclosure used by drovers to impound their cattle while spending the night in the village.

The White Horse Inn is the oldest of the two public houses in Castle Pulverbatch and was licensed in 1821. In 1901 the owners of the inn were Southam's Brewery from Shrewsbury. The landlord was William Cox and the house consisted of a bar, two parlours, a clubroom, six bedrooms, a main kitchen, a back kitchen and a cellar. There was also ample stabling at the rear for 10 horses. Elsie sent this postcard on 25 August 1932 to a Mrs Wallach who lived in Preston. She writes: 'We have found this to be all we could desire. There is rest and peace here, beautiful country and the inn is most comfortable and the food – oh divine!!! I shall be fat, fat, fat! We are both very well and send our best love to you. Have marked our bedroom with a cross. Elsie.' Note the petrol pump, the car hire sign and the inn sign advertising the brewery's 'Prize Medal Ales and Stout'.

Chapter Five
Military Matters

These troops are 'C' Squadron of the Ludlow Imperial Yeomanry, mustering in the outer bailey of the castle before setting off to war on 8 August 1914. Their call to arms was speedy and efficient, just four days after the outbreak of war. Their initial destination was a training camp at Oswestry before they were sent across country to East Anglia, where they were put on coastal defence duties.

The war memorial was unveiled around 1920 and until 1956 stood on the corner of the main A49 and the Corvedale Road. It was removed to Stokesay Churchyard during a road improvement scheme. The statue was nicknamed 'Old Bill' after the famous World War One cartoon character drawn by Bruce Bairnfather. Engraved on its sides are the names of the 24 men who died during World War One and of the eight men who perished in World War Two. The memorial also contains the names of 98 men, 'In grateful recognition of those of this parish who also fought for King and Country, happily returned'.

During World War Two there was quite an influx of military personnel in the town and a number of the larger houses in the area, as well as public buildings, were commandeered for military use. Like all areas of the country a Home Guard unit was formed in Craven Arms to help defend vital installations. These included the railway station, engine sheds and track that were used to take a huge volume of traffic through the town and south to Herefordshire, into mid-Wales and down to Swansea. When first formed the units were known as the Local Defence Volunteers or LDV for short, but when comedian Tommy Trinder said the initials stood for 'Look, Duck and Vanish', the more military title was adopted.

Hundreds of people line the road from Craven Arms Station to pay their last respects at this military funeral. The soldiers of the King's Shropshire Light Infantry, with their rifles reversed, lead the gun carriage and coffin away from the station towards the town. The station was the site of a serious accident in July 1907 when Walter Powell of Clun fell from scaffolding and died later from his injuries. Part of the scaffolding collapsed as he and his father were constructing it and it was alleged at the inquest that the poles and the planks were old and worn and that the scaffolding had not been erected correctly. The jury returned a verdict of accidental death, but added a rider that in their opinion the scaffolding had not been strong enough.

Walcot Park near Lydbury North covers over 1,000 acres and is almost surrounded by a circle of hills. At one time a huge herd of deer roamed the park, but these were moved to Powis Castle in 1813. The Earl of Powis, who was Lord Lieutenant of Shropshire, gave permission on two occasions in 1908 and 1912 for the annual camps of the Shropshire Imperial Yeomanry to be held there. The men in 1908 were mainly part-time soldiers from C Squadron based at Ludlow and from the Montgomeryshire Yeomanry. While at the camp they mounted roadblocks in the area, trained with musket and sword, improved their signalling techniques, attended lectures, drills and parades and took part in a variety of competitions and sporting activities.

On Sunday 17 May 1908 this Drum Service was held at Walcot Park for the Shropshire Yeomanry attending the annual camp. A.H. writes on the reverse of the card to Mrs Williams in Ashton Hayes, Chester: 'Have had good weather. Feeling at one.' The service was conducted by the Revd Hon. H.E. Lambard. The men looked splendid in their new uniforms and after the service the band played for the visitors to the park in the afternoon. After 1908 companies of the Shropshire Yeomanry and the Shropshire Royal Horse Artillery formed part of the Welsh Border Mounted Brigade.

Another service is held at the camp at Walcot, but this time with more civilians present on the bank overlooking the camp. The padre is standing just to the left of the band. A.H. writes on the back of this card to Miss Williams of West View, Broseley Wood: 'Do try and come up some day and spend a few hours. Thursday would be nice, if not try the following Wednesday. The little girl on the front of this PC with the white hat and coat is Lady Mona the Earl of Powis' daughter.'

The Duke of Wellington has been quoted as saying that an army marches on its stomach. If that is the case the troops camping at Walcot Park in May 1908 would have been able to put in a great deal of mileage. These men from the cookhouse pose proudly with their pots, pans, spoons, milk churns and tea urn during a short break. Note the sergeant on the left with his stripes sewn on to his white overall. On the reverse of the post card A.H. again writes to Miss Williams at West View, Broseley: 'H sends you this. We have been to Bishop's Castle today. Had a jolly day yesterday. Post coming, love to all A.H.'

This photograph was taken at Walcot Park in 1912 by M. Strawson, whose family ran a chemist's shop in Bishop's Castle. The rider is E. Hamar from the Ludlow-based C Squadron of the Shropshire Imperial Yeomanry. At the beginning of the 20th century their headquarters were at 2 The Trio, St Julian's Road, Ludlow. Major F. Hurt-Sitwell was the commanding officer, with Captain H. Gurney as his deputy. The drill sergeant was Squadron Sergeant-Major W. Middleton. In case of emergencies each mounted trooper had a small pouch containing a horseshoe attached to the side of his saddle, similar to a spare wheel for a car. Such camps would also have their own portable blacksmith's shop to attend to the constant needs of the horses.

Watched by the vicar, the Revd R. Machen, a young girl presents the Countess of Powis with a bouquet of flowers after she had opened the Patriotic Sale at Clun on 8 September 1915. Like so many communities around the country during World War One the people of Clun held events to raise money for the men fighting in the trenches and also to boost the morale of those left at home. Although the event looks as though it is being held in a farmyard, the presence of the Countess of Powis has encouraged everyone to turn out in their Sunday best. The legend between the two patriotic posters on the wall at the rear reads, 'It's Our Flag, Fight For It, Work For It'.

The war memorial in memory of the men from Clun who were killed in World War One was unveiled on 5 June 1921. It is built out of grey Cornish granite and carries the names of 30 men from World War One, seven from World War Two and one from the conflict in Northern Ireland, all of whom were killed on active service, inscribed on its base. The memorial stands just to the right of the lych gate that had been repaired and tidied up for the occasion. The lych gate was erected in about 1723, has four gables and is built out of wood with stone tiles. In 1839 it was sold to a local gentleman who used it as an arbour in his garden. A few years later the curate, the Revd E.C. Swainson, retrieved the gate, but the parishioners would not allow him to restore it to its original site as they preferred the more convenient access next to the Six Bells Inn. However, they allowed the curate to resite it at the west end of the churchyard to keep the cows away. In 1877 the gate was finally restored to its original site.

Like every other town and village in the country, Clun held its Peace Day to celebrate the ending of World War One on 5 August 1919. The event at Clun took the shape of a huge carnival parade and entertainment on the Castle Ground, similar to the annual Clun Show. The parade was headed by Minnie Gittins on horseback, dressed in a long white flowing dress, crown and a shoulder sash with 'peace' emblazoned across the front. She was flanked by Susan Roberts and Norah Morris, also mounted on horses and dressed as a soldier and a sailor. They were followed by a long parade of wagons and people, many dressed in patriotic style. This group includes Britannia in the centre with her trident and shield surrounded by our allies, including the US to her left, draped in the Stars and Stripes.

This is Church Parade in July 1909, on the camping ground at Church Stretton, which was just north of the town. The services always attracted a number of local people and one of the girls on the left is called Grace. The padre is the Revd Osman. As well as the infantry, men of the Shropshire Artillery Volunteers have also made use of the local amenities, making the top of the Long Mynd a firing range for their big guns. Cannon balls and pieces of shell are still found today on the sides of the hills by metal detecting enthusiasts. In the background are the Stretton hills.

The bugles and band of the King's Shropshire Light Infantry lead the men through the streets of Church Stretton in July 1909. Their march down Sandford Avenue brought out a large excited crowd to watch this fine spectacle, as Aunt Gertie relates to Master Smith on the reverse of the postcard: 'My dear old Jim. We have 500 soldiers here. It is a right sight to see them have their dinner. We went to see them yesterday. This is them going to the station. They are going to play on the green this evening. Love and Kisses from Auntie Gertie'. The young lime trees on both sides of the road were a gift from the Sandford Avenue Committee and were planted in the 1880s. Several of the trees were dedicated to people, including one to the Prince of Wales, which was planted in March 1885.

The photographer is looking across the open field towards the Camping Ground just to the north of Church Stretton, where the men of the First Battalion of the King's Shropshire Light Infantry have made their camp. The mess tents and cookhouse are on the left and the soldiers have pitched their own tents in perfectly straight lines in the centre. The latrines are on the right and the officers' tents are at the top, away from the other ranks. The men standing at the top of the first row of tents have laid their kit out for inspection and seem to be in their underwear. On Thursday 1 July 1909 the regiment was carrying out manoeuvres in the hills, similar to fighting guerrillas in India. Two days earlier they had completed a stiff hill march of 13 miles over some of the Long Mynd's toughest terrain. In the background is the Long Mynd and the entrance to Cardingmill Valley. The road at the top left is the Burway leading up to the summit. The houses on the right are on Trevor Hill with the Golf Club pavilion at the top. Note the large water pump in front of the tents with the notice advertising 'Stretton Waters'.

At the outbreak of World War One a great wave of patriotism swept over the country and thousands of young men rushed to join the army. Many regiments of 'Pals' were formed in the larger cities and towns to fight in a conflict they were convinced would be over by Christmas. These men are all recruits from Munslow in the Corvedale who volunteered to join the army on 1 September 1914. Ominously on the war memorial there are nine names of men from the village that died in the trenches, which makes you wonder how many of these men who volunteered during the first month of the war survived, and whether the little girl ever got her father back.

In the shadow of Pontesford Hill the men of the Shropshire Imperial Yeomanry pitch their tents for their annual camp in 1907. As well as using the facilities at Pontesford, other camps were held at Walcot Park near Lydbury North, Brogyntyn Park at Oswestry and Attingham Park at Atcham in the early years of the 20th century. The men were drilled at Longden Manor and manoeuvres were held on Pontesford and Cothercott Hills and over the rough terrain of the Stiperstones. The total strength of the camp was 459 men divided into four squadrons. They were under the command of Colonel Lord Kenyon, who had just taken over from Lord Harlech. His second-in-command was Lt.-Col Sir Walter Corbet. Mr Swire of Longden Manor put the camping ground, which was just 10 minutes walk from Plealey Road Station, at their disposal.

This is another view of the Shropshire Imperial Yeomanry Camp at Pontesford in 1907. These camps took a great deal of organisation to cater for the men and horses over a two-week period. The *Chronicle* described the camp in this way: 'Good and ample accommodation for the Headquarters is afforded amidst delightful surroundings which make the camp one of the most pleasantest the Regiment has known'. Note the neat rows of tents for the men, the mess tents to the right and the picket line of horses in the foreground. On Thursday 16 May, just two days after their arrival, a serious accident occurred when Private Heighway of 'A' Squadron was thrown from his horse. He had just commenced drilling the horse when it was frightened by a passing car, causing it to panic. Private Heighway fell heavily, receiving a compound fracture to his elbow, which needed hospital treatment at the Salop Infirmary.

These men, dressed in the blue patrol uniforms of the Imperial Shropshire Yeomanry, are exercising in the grounds of Longden Manor near Pontesbury. The surrounding hills were also easily adapted for the manoeuvres of mounted infantry. The first of two large exercises took place at the camp on the Friday, when the troops had to form a chain of outposts that would warn headquarters of enemy troops approaching from Shifnal. For this exercise the Wellington Imperial Yeomanry acted as the enemy. On the second exercise it was reported that 5,000 enemy troops had landed in Aberystwyth and were marching on Welshpool. With the help of regular troops from the KSLI the enemy were captured and both manoeuvres were considered a success. The men trained as mounted infantrymen and were affiliated to the Corps of Dragoons.

Drills, night manoeuvres and surprise attacks were organised in Walcot Park and a mock battle was also staged on the Long Mynd and surrounding neighbourhood. An accident occurred during one of the exercises that cast gloom over the entire camp. During troop drill Trooper Fitton of Whitchurch was badly hurt after his horse put a foot down a rabbit hole. The horse did a complete somersault, rolled over the rider three times and dragged him along the ground for several yards before kicking him in the head. He was taken unconscious to the hospital tent where first aid was administered. In consideration of Trooper Fitton's condition the band did not play in the mess tent at dinner and all bugle calls were stopped.

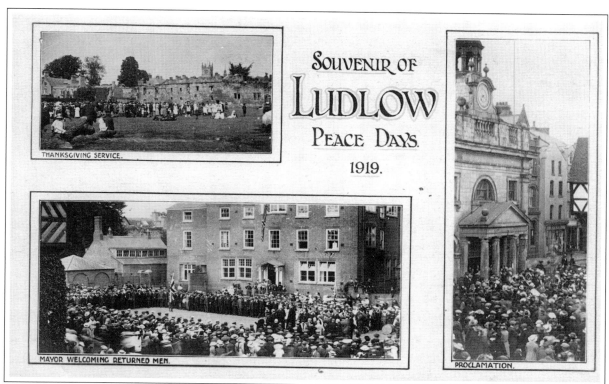

During July and August 1919 towns and villages all over the country held Peace Days to welcome home servicemen who had fought in World War One. Ludlow held their Peace Day on 19 July and the town was tastefully decorated with flags, mottoes and streamers. At 6am maroons were fired from the Castle Green to wake the people of Ludlow and the bells of the church began ringing at 6.30am. The bugle band of the Ludlow KRR Cadets paraded through the streets of the town and at 9am the children's sports began on the Castle Green, attracting 1,148 competitors. A short service of thanksgiving was led by the Revd A.E. Lloyd Kenyon and the Revd W.F. Taylor before the Mayor, Ald. E. Sheldon, planted a Victory Oak on Castle Walk. At 12.30pm the Mayor and Corporation, headed by the bugle band, marched to the Castle Square to welcome home 500 active and demobilised soldiers and sailors. After the ceremony they all processed to the Town Hall where the men were entertained to dinner. During the afternoon a children's tea party was held, but the men's athletics events were postponed until Saturday morning due to heavy rain.

The Shropshire Imperial Yeomanry held their annual camp at Walcot Park in May 1912. Some of the squadrons travelled by train to Craven Arms but the Shrewsbury Squadron marched all the way from the county town, arriving at the camp by 4.30pm. The tents had been erected before the men arrived so after feeding and watering their horses they were able to dine themselves. Col. Lord Kenyon was in command of the camp, which consisted of 24 officers, 410 men and 390 horses. Many of the men were very well mounted on their own horses, which were worth in the region of £100 each. The first day at the camp was devoted to drill in the park and an inspection by Brigadier Herbert of Chester, who expressed great satisfaction with the regiment.

Chapter Six
Churches and Chapels

E.E. Miller of 19 Corve Street Ludlow published this view of the entrance to the new cemetery at Henley Road, Ludlow. The Bishop of Hereford consecrated the new cemetery on Friday 5 March 1915. The ground had been provided by the Town Council, which had secured the site in 1914 for £750. The bishop was met at the main entrance and the petition for consecrating the ground was read out to him by Mr C.B. Beddoes, the Diocesan Registrar. A procession walked around the new ground and was led by the Town Crier, Mr H. Morgan. The choir, the bishop and local clergy, the mace bearer, the Mayor and rector and other council officials followed him. The choir sang the 21st Psalm and the Bishop offered up prayers and gave a short address.

Bromfield Church lies close to the River Onny and is approached through this splendid lych gate. There was a collegiate church on this site in Saxon times with 12 canons. By the 12th century a Benedictine priory had been established and was there until 1540 when it was dissolved and the land transferred to Charles Foxe, who transformed parts of the priory into a house. The church is dedicated to St Mary and services were restored in 1658. The tower is a mixture of architectural styles; the lower section is in an Early English style while the battlements are Perpendicular and date from about 1300.

This is another view from the east of the church of St Mary at Bromfield. The chancel has a painted ceiling, which was the work of Cheshire-born artist Thomas Francis. It depicts angels and clouds, with streamers bearing religious texts, and was executed in 1672. The church also contains a memorial to Dr Henry Hickman, the pioneer of anaesthetics, who was born at Lady Halton near Bromfield. On the left is the gatehouse of the old Benedictine priory that was suppressed by Henry VIII in 1540. It was built of broad stone with a timber-framed upper storey and gable that dates from the 14th century. In the past it has been used as a village school and as a reception room.

The church at Hopesay is dedicated to St Mary and dates mainly from around 1200. The tower is squat and defensive and has a double pyramid roof, very similar to the church of St George at Clun. In the 15th century the nave was given a beautifully panelled roof of Spanish chestnut. The old stone rectory stands just behind the church. Towards the end of the 19th and into the 20th century the rectory was home to several incumbents, the most notable being the Revd Augustus Field MA of Clare College, Cambridge, who was described as rector and rural dean of Bishop's Castle in 1900 and prebendary of Hereford and rector and rural dean of Clun in 1905.

The church at Bucknell was dedicated to St Mary and was erected in the 12th century, but little remains of the old building as it was greatly restored in 1870. During the alterations, which cost about £2,000, the high pews and the gallery were removed and the north aisle, vestry and organ chamber were added. All that remains of the original church is a blocked priests' door in the south wall of the chancel and an arch on the north wall. The church has an attractive wooden tower at the west end that contains a clock and a peal of three bells. The oldest dates from 1684 and has the names of the churchwardens, John Gretton and Francis Matthews, inscribed on it.

This is the tranquil view from the lych gate of St Mary's Church in Bucknell to the Church Bridge over the Redlake River. Although the church is of no great age it does have an 11th-century carved font. The carved head is thought to date from the Norman period but the pattern work is older and dates from Saxon times. The church and the village school are closely linked and in the past, on 6 December, all the pupils would take part in a play about St Nicholas, followed by a Boy Bishop Service at the church. At the service one of the boys would dress up as St Nicholas and at the end he would distribute little bags of sweets to the children in the congregation. Cranage described the lych gate as having an unusual swinging door and dating from around 1900.

The Bishop's Castle Primitive Methodist Church stands in Station Road. It was erected in 1904 at a cost of around £1,500, with seating for 200 worshippers. It stands as a testament to the earlier travelling preachers who risked life and limb to bring religion to the people of a town that was often known in the middle of the 19th century as the 'Devil's Mansion' or 'Little Sodom'. Two Primitive Methodist preachers visited Bishop's Castle on 10 August 1828 and began preaching to a small group on Castle Green. Soon a large mob arrived and began to jeer and throw stones

at them. Several tried to grab hold of them and they would have been ejected from the town if a local prizefighter had not threatened to knock down any man that laid a hand on them. During the afternoon they began preaching again, but this time the mob proved too fierce and after a short while they were forced to flee across the fields under a hail of missiles.

Bishop's Castle Congregational Church was opened in New Street on 23 July 1913, with space to accommodate 250 worshippers. It replaced the old building erected in Chapel Yard in 1807 with seating for 120 people. The old chapel was later converted into the town library. Two services connected to the opening were held on 10 August when the Revd Townsend from Bridgnorth gave the sermons. Miss Williams of Shrewsbury was the soloist for the day and in the morning sang *The Better Land* and in the evening *The Heavenly Song*. During the evening service the choir under Mr S. Bennett, the organist and choirmaster, rendered the anthem *King of Kings*. The collection at both services amounted to £3 18s, which was given to the building fund. One of the highlights for the children in the early part of the 20th century was the weekly meeting of the Band of Hope, which was non-denominational. At each meeting groups from the church and the three chapels would meet and be given time to put together a programme of items that would be performed at a monthly concert.

Mainstone lies three miles south-west of Bishop's Castle in the wooded valley of the River Unk. The name of the village is thought to derive from the Welsh 'maen' denoting a stone or from 'maeganstan' meaning a great stone. The church is dedicated to St John the Baptist and lies about a mile outside the village. Offa's Dyke runs just to the west of the churchyard and the church is often referred to as 'the church on the Dyke'. Within the church is a large granite rock weighing around 200 pounds. No one seems to know its origin but it has been suggested that it was used to test a young man's strength or as a measure to weigh corn. This church was almost entirely rebuilt in 1887. One of the most important days for the villagers was Harvest Festival, when the church would be packed for the two services.

The church at Bishop's Castle lies at the bottom of the hill at the southern end of the town and is dedicated to St John the Baptist. The church was built in 1291 but the main body of the building was destroyed by fire in 1645 during the Civil War, although the tower survived. During the Victorian alterations an early English doorway was removed from the building and has been incorporated into the wall of the vicarage garden. In the churchyard is the grave of Lt. Col. Louis Pace of the French Light Cavalry, who died on 1 May 1814 while being held in the town as a prisoner of war. There are also records of babies being fathered by other French prisoners on parole! These men were allowed to walk unguarded to a white post set up on the outside of the town. The distance between the posts was known as 'The Frenchman's Mile'.

Lydbury North lies three miles south-east of Bishop's Castle. It was mentioned in the Domesday Survey and was one of the most important settlements in the area until it was overtaken by Bishop's Castle in the 12th century. The church is dedicated to St Michael and All Angels and dates mainly from the Norman period. Its tower, with walls several feet thick, reflects the closeness of the Welsh border and the need for defence in times of trouble. Today the tower contains a clock and a peal of six bells, three dating from 1660 but recast in 1870. The church is unusual as it contains a Roman Catholic chapel within the fabric of an Anglican church. It was built by the Plowden family, who were devout Catholics, on the north side of the chancel. It was erected in memory of the safe return of Roger Plowden after his escape from the city of Acre during one of the Crusades.

In 1914 the tower and the bell caps of St George's Church in Clun were repaired and the six old bells were sent to London to be recast. After their removal from the tower they were taken by wagon to the station at Broome where they were loaded onto a train for their journey up to the capital. The men are, from the left: George Drinkwater, the Revd Machen, vicar of Clun, Joe Luther the maltster, R. Davies from the mill, William Mead the grocer and ironmonger and Bill Morris. The man sitting among the bells is D. Davies and the young boy under the lych gate is Frankie Morgan.

The recast bells, plus two new ones, arrived by rail at Broome Station on 22 July 1914, which turned out to be a lovely summer day. Two wagons were needed to return the bells to Clun and this was done with great ceremony. The wagons were decorated with laurel, yew and roses and the Revd Harold Scott, carrying a wooden cross, led the parade. He was followed by the children from Clun School and their teachers, Mr Frank Short and Mrs Cleeton. Mr Tong led the choir, who were followed by a number of local clergymen, the parish council, the churchwardens and the bells on the wagons. Bringing up the rear were the almsmen wearing their blue cloaks and high hats.

During the parade back to Clun several hymns were sung, accompanied by one of the choir playing a cornet. When they arrived at Clun the whole town gathered around the entrance to the church to watch the safe return of the bells. The choir assembled under the lych gate and the schoolchildren lined up on the church wall with their banners proclaiming, 'Welcome The Bells', 'Pease Be Unto Clun', and 'God Bless The Bells'. The Revd Machen spoke to the crowd and prayed for the bells before everyone adjourned to the vicarage garden for tea and games.

The bells are displayed outside the west door of St George's Church, Clun, with local clergy and gentlemen. The two new bells are on the left with the six recast bells on the right. The inscriptions on the old bells are, 'John Latward Richard Bowen Wardens 1681 Part Of This Is The Gift Of Joseph Jactson', 'All Prayse And Glory Be To God For Ever T.P.E.B.C.W. of Clun 1668', 'Jesus Be Our Good Speed 1668', 'Sing We Merrily Peace Be To Clun 1668', 'Soli Deo Gloria Pax Hominibvs 1668', 'God Save The King. Thomas Powell. Edward Bowen. C.W. 1668'. The inscription on the first new bell reads 'To The Glory Of God And In Memory Of Clara Creswell Who Died July 17, 1886'. The second new bell was inscribed with the name of the vicar, the Revd R. Machen, and the two churchwardens, Mr G. Townsend and Mr W. Darroll. At a funeral the bells were muffled but at a bell-ringer's funeral his bell was muffled but the others were not. From left to right are: Revd Vaughn, Mr W. Mead, Revd H. Scott, Mr G. Townsend, Revd R. Machen, Mr Darroll, Mr J. Davies, -?-, Revd Cope.

A respectful group of onlookers watch as the vicar, choir and congregation of St George's Church parade around Clun on Church Day in June 1921. The vicar is the Revd Maurice Bonner Lutener, who had only taken up the post the previous year. The parade marched down to the river near the castle and an outdoor service was held there. Note the banner at the rear of the parade depicting St George, the Patron Saint of England, slaying the dragon. The crowd are standing outside the remains of the Six Bells, which was burnt down in January 1915.

The first Primitive Methodist travelling preachers tried to hold open-air missionary services at Clun as early as 1828 but all their attempts ended with them either retreating under a hail of missiles or being manhandled out of town. The Shrewsbury Circuit Plan for March 1832 shows that many of the surrounding villages were being missioned, including Clunton and Clungunford, but Clun was missed out. However, over the next three years rapid progress was made with a chapel opening on 4 January 1835 and a Sunday school with 133 pupils and six teachers opening in 1837. The Primitives seemed to flourish more than the Wesleyans. This chapel, which could seat 250, was erected on the corner of the High Street and Hospital Lane in 1878 for about £1,000. The large chapel manse at the rear was built in Hospital Lane in 1887 to accommodate the resident preacher and his family.

The church of St Swithin at Clunbury dates from the Norman period. The nave is the oldest part of the building, closely followed by the lower part of the tower, the upper section having been rebuilt in the 17th century. The south porch is Victorian and would have been built around the time that the church was restored in 1881 for about £1,654. A new clock was fitted into the tower in 1900 at a cost of £72. Inside the church there is a Norman font and some nice stained glass, including a window in the south of the nave by Kempe.

The church at Clungunford lies at the bottom of the village near the river and the remains of the old castle mound. The church dates mainly from the 13th century and is dedicated to St Cuthbert. E. Turner of Leicester heavily restored it at the end of the 19th century and it was at this time that the tower and porch were added. The tower contains a clock, which was the gift of W.W.G. Hurt-Sitwell, and three bells. J.C.L. Rocke gave the organ to the church in 1895. Until 1636 it was the custom for the rector to supply the poor and elderly of the village with bread, cheese and ale on Easter Sunday. When the custom was stopped angry parishioners petitioned the church authorities to overturn the decision, but they refused.

This is the southern end of the High Street in Church Stretton, looking north towards Shrewsbury. Joseph Bratton from Birkenhead designed the Congregational Church on the right. It cost around £1,000, which was raised by public subscription, and was opened on 19 May 1866 with seating for 200 people. The building was overhauled in 1886 and again in 1937. A preacher's house was built in 1909 and a church hall in 1957. In 1972 it became a United Reformed Church after the Congregational Church united with the Presbyterian Church. The people at the top of the street are outside the Queen's Head Inn, a building that dates from about 1820. The inn closed and is now the home of Church Stretton's two Masonic Lodges.

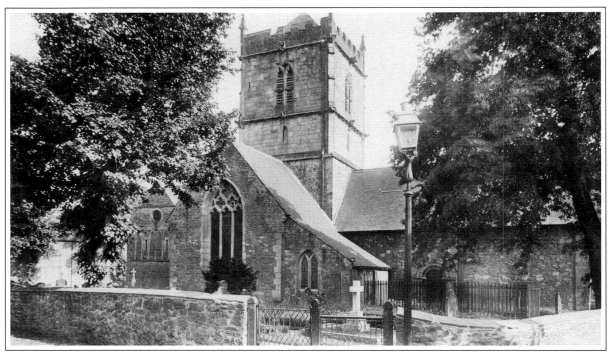

The church dedicated to St Laurence in Church Stretton is built on the site of a Saxon church. The nave is Norman but the chancel, transept and tower are later. The tower contains eight bells, six cast by Abraham Rudhall in 1711 and two more added later. This message to bell ringers was placed in the belfry in 1773: 'If you ring and do come here, You must ring well with hand and ear, And if the bell you over throw, 4d to pay before you go, and if you ring in spur and hat, 6d you must pay for that, or in this place you swear and curse, 12d to pay pull out your purse.' The chiming clock was a gift from the rector, the Revd C. Noel Hill, in 1890.

All Saints' Church in Little Stretton was built as a chapel of ease and paid for by Mrs Gibbon, who lived in the Manor House. Despite the old rustic appearance it was opened just over a century ago on 20 October 1903. It is an iron structure, ornamented in wood to give it a timber-framed appearance. It was bought from a firm in Manchester specialising in this type of building and assembled by local workmen. The thatched roof was added in 1935 and was paid for by Derwent Wood, an artist who lived at the Old Tan House. As well as the church there was also a Primitive Methodist chapel and a Wesleyan chapel in the village.

At the beginning of the 20th century the area around Church Stretton was becoming popular as a holiday resort and as a place to retire. New places of worship were required and this church, dedicated to St Michael and All Angels, was consecrated as a chapel of ease in All Stretton on 24 October 1902. The money to build the church was raised by the Revd R.C. Noel Hill, the rector of Church Stretton, partly from the parish and partly from friends outside the parish. The building was designed by the diocesan architect Mr Arthur Lloyd Oswell, and consists of a small apsed chancel, nave, south transept, bell tower and porch. It was built out of locally quarried Long Mynd stone with Grinshill stone dressing.

This is a good view of the western tower of St James' Church in Cardington, seen from across the graveyard. The building on the right is the village school, which was founded after a charity was set up in the will of William Hall, dated April 1720. The charity stipulated that the schoolmaster must be a member of the Church of England, of good character and must have a female assistant to teach sewing. Pupils were to be between the ages of four and 14 and were to be taught the three Rs and the girls sewing. The pupils also had to attend church and 'behave decently'; if they did not they were to be punished by the master. The old school was condemned by the Education Department in 1871 and a new one was opened on part of the old site in 1873 with room for 120 pupils. The village has now lost its school and the building has been converted into a house.

These youngsters are sitting on the wall of the Congregational Chapel in Pontesbury in about 1910. The chapel was erected in 1836 with seating for 200 worshippers. It was the second non-conformist church to be erected in the village. The first was the Baptist Chapel, opened in 1828, again with accommodation for 200 people. Both chapels also had a minister's house and their own graveyard. Two more chapels for the Primitive and the Wesleyan Methodists were built in the village at a later date. Perhaps the boy on the right holding the brush hook had been tidying up the graveyard.

Habberley is situated one and a half miles south of Pontesbury. The church dedicated to St Mary is small and consists of a chancel, nave and a western tower containing two bells. The church dates from Norman times but has been rebuilt over the years using the old masonry. It was completely reroofed and repaired in 1864 and new seating was put in. The church also contains two nice stained-glass windows. The one at the east end is a memorial to Frederick Sparrow, who died in 1868, while the one in the west end, erected in 1881, is in memory of Helen Bowen, the wife of the Revd F.G.A. Bowen, who died at Arrah in Bengal in India.

Wesleyan Methodists in Hanwood first met in the room of a house in Weir Road that had been built by John Marshall as a lodging house for single male employees. As the congregation grew a new chapel was built in 1911 at the western end of the village near the railway bridge and was opened on 19 September 1912. The land was given by Samuel Atherton, the owner of the Hanwood coalmine and brickworks. Mrs Atherton laid the foundation stone and the building was erected out of Hanwood brick and a stone dressing. The new chapel cost £756, which included a schoolroom, kitchen, vestry and porch. The money was raised locally with people buying bricks at 2s 6d each. Owing to dwindling congregations the chapel closed in 1968 and like so many old chapels and schools it was converted into two houses in 1972.

Shrewsbury Primitive Methodist Circuit sent travelling preachers out to mission Minsterley with great success from the early 1830s. It became a Branch in 1839 and was judged big enough by 1851 to send its own reports to the District Meeting. The Minsterley Branch continued to flourish and was made into a separate Circuit in 1856, by which time they could boast 208 full members and 30 local preachers, but only one travelling preacher. The number of chapels or preaching rooms had grown to six while they had another 12 places on the preaching plan. The most outstanding feature of their success was the number of Sunday Schools they ran. In 1856 they had seven schools on their books, run by 62 teachers and attended by no less than 393 children. By the look of this photograph the success continued into the 20th century.

The name Pontesbury is thought to mean 'the fort in the hollow or valley'. The parish church is dedicated to St George and lies roughly at the centre of a modern road system that encircles the building. The chancel is built out of sandstone and dates from the 13th century, but the tower and nave were rebuilt in 1829 following the collapse of the old tower. The new tower contains a clock and six bells. The architect for the rebuilding was John Turner of Whitchurch. St George's was once a collegiate church with a dean and three canons.

Baptists in the Stiperstones area met for many years in the local blacksmith's shop until the Lord's Hill Baptist Church was built on a remote hillside in about 1833. In 1873 the chapel was rebuilt with a minister's house at the side. The author Mary Webb used the chapel in her book *Gone to Earth*, calling the area 'God's Little Mountain'. A film was made of the book in 1950 starring Jennifer Jones, Cyril Cusak and Dame Sybil Thorndike. Many scenes were shot in the area and the chapel became one of the central locations for the film, with Cyril Cusak playing the part of the minister Edward Marston. Many local people took part in the film when they were hired to dress up in Victorian attire as extras.

In 1913 the Liberal Government led by the Welsh Prime Minister David Lloyd George introduced a bill to Parliament, which would lead to the disestablishment of the Welsh Church. The Welsh Bill, as it became known, was extremely controversial and brought out feelings of overwhelming hostility among the English. To fight the bill and to make the feelings of the people known, mass meetings and rallies were held throughout the country. On 2 July 1913 a mass protest meeting against the Welsh Bill was held at Stokesay Castle. The meeting was organised by the Archdeaconry of Ludlow Church Defence Committee and attracted over 1,100 people with representatives from Bishop's Castle, Clun, Burford, Church Stretton and Ludlow. The meeting was presided over by the Earl of Powis and the main speakers were the Venerable Archdeacon Oldham, Dean of St Asaph, the Revd W.M.D. La Touche and Mr Mervyn Price. The meeting began with the hymn *O God Our Help in Ages Past* and prayers led by the Revd Cole-Hamilton, the vicar of Stokesay. After three passionate speeches against the bill the Revd Lloyd-Kenyon, rector of Ludlow, thanked the speakers for 'giving it to them hot and strong' and said he trusted that the meeting would make a difference to the vote in Parliament. The meeting broke up after the singing of the hymn *Praise God from whom All Blessings Flow* and the National Anthem, both of which were accompanied by a cornet player. The meetings did bring about a number of minor amendments but the bill became law in 1914, leading to the disestablishment of the Church of Wales on 31 March 1920. Standing on the platform, from the left, are: the cornet player, Revd Cole-Hamilton, Revd Lloyd-Kenyon, Ven. Archdeacon Oldham, Revd La Touché, Earl of Powis and Mr Mervyn Price.

It seemed to be the custom in this area of south Shropshire to erect triumphal arches along the route taken by a local dignitary and his bride on their return home from honeymoon. This was one of many, set out along the road from Aston-on-Clun to the Rectory at Clungunford, to greet the Revd William Rocke and his new wife, the former Miss Charlotte Artindale. They were greeted by a large crowd of residents who escorted them to their home. About a quarter of a mile from the rectory the horses were removed from the carriage and many willing hands quickly towed the vehicle to their destination. In 1898 a similar event occurred for the rector of Hopesay and his new bride. As well as the arches, one with the motto written in Gaelic in honour of the rector's homeland, fireworks were fired from Rectory Wood. So pleased with their welcome were the rector and his new wife that they invited the whole parish to tea the following Tuesday. Over 600 sat down to the meal, which featured 'Buzzard's wedding cake'. This was followed by sports and, in the evening, dancing to the Clun Town Band. The motto over this arch reads, 'As happy as the bridal morn, may the evening of your life be'.

Chapter Seven
Recreation and Rural Tranquillity

A gentleman with binoculars takes advantage of the panoramic views available from the Whitcliffe on a clear day, while a courting couple sit quietly surveying the scene across the river to the town. The name Whitcliffe is derived from 'white cliff' and refers to the limestone found there, which over the centuries has been quarried for building material by the people of Ludlow. The cliff was formed by the receding Ice Age, when melting water wore away the limestone to create this gorge between the Whitcliffe and the town. As well as quarrying, the area has been used for grazing animals and leisure, with locals and tourists walking and picnicking there. The hillside furnishes the visitor with a fine view over Ludlow and an outlook over the Stretton Hills, Wenlock Edge and the Clee Hills.

There has been horse racing on the Old Field at Bromfield since the 1720s. At first races were promoted by Henry Herbert of Oakley Park, who also paid for the lavish balls and entertainment held in the evenings following the races. In 1871 the Race Club was inaugurated, with members having to pay an annual subscription of £5 plus an entrance fee of £5. Membership of the club was limited to 400 and in 1907, the year when the new grandstand was opened, the membership stood at 360. At this time the course was one and a half miles and 114 yards long and was known as 'the Northern Sandown'. On the reverse of the postcard is this message to Mrs F. Bastin of Cheltenham: 'This is the new grandstand at the last meeting, a great many more people than when you last saw it.' In May 1907 Fred Warton, alias 'Askey', a bookmaker from Birmingham, was accused of stealing six shillings at the course by 'Welshing'. A gentleman from Richard's Castle had laid the bet at 3 to 1 on a horse called Snuff. The horse won but when he went to collect his winnings the bookmaker had disappeared. The criminal was apprehended by the police as he made his way to the railway station.

A group of Edwardian ladies enjoy a visit to Ludlow Castle, escorted round by the guide on the left wearing the straw boater. The group have climbed to the top of the keep and are looking back towards the outer bailey. Behind them to the right is the Great Chamber block; the Great Hall is in the centre with part of the solar on the left. The keep is of Norman origin and has been greatly altered over a number of years. The domestic range dates from the 13th century and was again altered at various times to add more comfort for the inhabitants. Soon after the Council of the Marches was disbanded in 1689 it fell into disrepair and was described by the author Daniel Defoe, when he visited Ludlow 33 years later in 1722, as being 'in the very perfection of decay'.

Archery would have been practised in the outer bailey of the castle for centuries. It seems to have been a popular pastime for ladies in the late 19th and early 20th century, as a photograph of another group of ladies, from the Cambrian Archaeological Society, are shown shooting from that same spot at their meeting in August 1898. A local group who practised there were the Archers of the Teme. During a match in 1908 the gentlemen shot six dozen arrows at 60 yards while the ladies shot the National Round. Mrs Lewis with 235 points and seven golds achieved the highest score for the ladies. Mr Fixsen won the men's match with 245 points and five golds. Behind is the massive Norman keep, to the left the Oven Tower and to the right the Judge's Lodgings. Over the entrance are the arms of England and France on the top shield and those of Queen Elizabeth I and Sir Henry Sidney below. They are dated 1581 and were erected at the same time as the building by Sir Henry, who had been President of the Council since 1560.

Three ladies enjoy a rest on the Castle Walk outside Ludlow Castle at the beginning of the 20th century. The path was laid out around 1772, as a fashionable walk for the gentry of Ludlow to promenade beneath the massive walls of the castle and to enjoy the fine views across the River Teme to the Whitcliffe. The round tower is known as Mortimer's Tower and was built in the early 13th century. It is thought to have contained a gateway leading into the outer bailey. In the late 16th century Sir Henry Sidney altered the tower into a store for the old records of the Council of the Marches.

The train pulling into Bucknell Station is heading towards Craven Arms. The people waiting on the platform are all dressed up and are perhaps going on an excursion to Shrewsbury Flower Show, which attracted hundreds of visitors by rail from all over the county and from Wales. The wooden waiting room on this side of the track does not compare very well with the ornate stone station house on the left. The billboard on the wall is advertising outings on the London and North Western Railway to pleasure resorts such as Ilfracombe, while Pears Soap offers you a 'Matchless Complexion'.

The Lingen Bridge crosses the River Teme half a mile south of Bucknell. A local carpenter called Morris erected the first bridge at this natural crossing in 1770. As it was a popular crossing for coaches and wagons, it was suggested in 1828 that the county authorities take responsibility for its upkeep or replacement. After a great deal of negotiation and a contribution of £150 by the local gentry, James Cole, a builder from Presteigne, was chosen by the county to build the new bridge. It was a timber structure placed on three piers, two made of wood and the third from stone. By 1837 repairs had to be carried out on the foundations at a cost of £310. The old bridge was replaced by this 32ft-long metal structure, resting on stone piers, which was built by the Coalbrookdale Company and completed in 1877.

This photograph was taken from the back of Walcot Hall and shows the wood laid out on the hillside to spell the name Plassey. This was the scene of Lord Clive's greatest victory in 1759 and the battle that helped to make India part of the British Empire. For many years it was a part of the landscape and admired by many visitors to the park. It was also well known by pilots and was used as a navigational aid. This, however, led to its removal during World War Two as it was thought that German aircrews could also use it as a reference point.

A young family pose outside the youth hostel on Mill Road, Clun. The hostel was set up in the early 1930s in a converted water mill that was used for grinding corn. The mill used the waters of the River Clun as a source of power. The river rises on the Welsh border and flows down to Clun where it is joined by the River Unk; it then flows south to join the River Teme at Leintwardine. In 1905 the mill belonged to Thomas Davies, who was listed as a baker and a grocer in the High Street and as a farmer and miller at Clun Mill. As late as 1951 the mill was not recommended for those people who wanted running water, electricity and modern conveniences, but for those who enjoyed getting involved in rural life. Both the girls' and men's dormitories were reached by ladder and the men's washroom was where the mill ponies used to be stabled, with the new white washbasins fitting neatly into the old drinking troughs.

The printer of this card has made a mistake with the spelling of the place name, which should read Woolbury Rock instead of Wollabury Rock. The site of the rock is well known to walkers and ramblers and sits on the western slope of the Black Hill one mile south-east of Clun. 'L', who sent this card to Miss E. Christian of Aberdeenshire, writes: 'This is a view of a secluded little spot near here, we made up a party and went for a climb to this place on the hill, the view was lovely'. In 1931 the father of Mrs Hall of Shrewsbury wrote to her from the Buffalo Hotel, Clun: 'Had a fine walk here to the Rock of Woolbury, a real bit of Derbyshire in Shropshire'.

The tiny hamlet of Bicton lies just one and a half miles north-west of Clun and has changed very little since this photograph was taken in the early years of the 20th century. The buildings sit at the foot of Bica's Hill, from which the name of the settlement is derived. The River Unk flows through the hamlet on its way to join the River Clun. Close by there is a castle mound that once guarded the valley and a wooden footbridge crosses the river by a timber-framed cottage. In *Kelly's Directory* for 1905 Edward Hamar, a farmer, is the only person listed at Bicton.

This footbridge was built over the River Onny just south of the village of Clunton. It was erected out of wood with just a stone pier in the centre and was built next to a natural ford. It is mentioned in the book *Ancient Bridges of Wales and Western England*, written by E. Jervoise in the 1920s. He believed that although most of the timbers of the bridge had just been renewed it was a very old bridge. This bridge was dismantled in about 1960 and replaced by a road bridge over the site of the ford where the horse and cart are crossing. The cottages, which were very prone to flooding, have also been demolished. The Thomas and Evans families were the last people to occupy the cottages.

Aston-on-Clun lies two miles west of Craven Arms and is a village of stone cottages and timber-framed houses. The stream that runs down Mill Street is a small tributary of the River Clun. Note the young man standing in the stream and the stone bridges that gave access to the cottages. In the early part of the 20th century the village was able to offer a number of facilities, including an inn, a tailor, a stone mason, a plumber and glazier and a post office run by the Whitefoot family, who also ran the village store from the same premises.

A young boy sits in the middle of a wooden footbridge over the River Clun, close to the tiny hamlet of Beckjay. The weir was built to maintain the height and flow of water to power the watermill that was used for grinding corn. The mill and a section of the waterwheel can just be seen on the right through the gap in the bushes. The scene is reminiscent of A.E. Houseman's poem, 'In valley of springs and rivers,/By Onny, and Teme and Clun,/The country for easy livers,/the quietest under the sun.'

The name Clungunford is derived from 'Clun', the river, 'Gunnas', a Saxon lord, and 'ford', a river crossing. Some of the children standing under the oak tree are obviously related to Willie Evans, who sent this postcard to his sister, who was in service with a Mr Beake who lived at Dinham in Ludlow. He writes, 'My dear sister, just a line to you as it leaves us all well at home. You are to notice who are on the card. Dad has been hurt with a horse this morning but it is not much, from Willie'.

Newcastle on Clun nestles among the hills in the beautiful Clun Valley three miles north-west of Clun. The village stands near the confluence of the River Clun and the Folly Brook, which has two arms, the main one rising by Long Pike Hollow near the Cantlin Stone and the other at Folly Bank. The millpond was built to provide a good head of water for the millrace that provides a torrent of water to work the wheel. The mill at Newcastle was used to grind corn.

Church Stretton Golf Club was opened by Vardon and Taylor in 1898 and was originally a nine-hole course, but facilities were soon upgraded to a full 18 holes. In 1905, gentlemen residents of Church Stretton paid an annual subscription of two guineas; non-residents and ladies paid one guinea. Visitor's fees were 2s 6d for one day, 7s 6d for a week or 20 shillings for a month. A special discount of half fees was given to all members of the same family after the first two. The clubhouse with the veranda, which had a superb view over the town, is on the left. The notice reads: 'Church Stretton Golf Club. Members Only. Trespassers Will Be Prosecuted. Dogs Not Allowed'.

Members of Church Stretton Golf Club have to be very fit to play a round of golf. The course is situated on the eastern side of the lower slopes of the Long Mynd, with the height of the course varying between 800ft and 1,000ft. The fairways are undulating and the turf is springy, which led golf legend Henry Cotton to describe it as 'real hill top golf'. Several greens are situated on the edge of steep slopes and many golf balls have frustrated players by ending up in the valley below. Every hole has a name, the first being the 'Rabbit Burrow'. At the beginning of the 20th century monthly competitions were held on the first Thursday of the month. It was reported that the weather for the competition held on 2 May 1907 was 'far from ideal' but the greens were in 'excellent condition'. The Revd A. Roberts won the competition from a handicap of 15; runner up on a handicap of three was W.S. Vivian.

Due to its location in the heart of the Shropshire hill country Church Stretton became known as 'Little Switzerland', 'The British Shangri-la', or the 'Highlands of England'. It boasted that it was strongly recommended by the medical profession for its 'magnificent scenery, pure air and water and equable climate'. The Chalet Pavilion was erected in the Cardingmill Valley to help cater for the influx of tourists. At weekends in the late 1950s and early 1960s hundreds of people would descend on Stretton from all over Shropshire and the West Midlands. For the active there were walks up to the Light Spout Waterfall, to Mott's Road or to the ancient Bodbury Ring. For the less energetic a quiet picnic by the stream or an ice cream and a nice cup of tea at the Chalet Pavilion was a pleasant way to spend an afternoon. To the side of the pavilion in the 1950s were a number of penny slot machines including three dedicated to 'What the Butler Saw'.

These Edwardian ramblers are having a well-earned rest before continuing their walk over the beautiful hills around Church Stretton. Many little booklets have been written over the years to encourage walkers to sample the delights of a stroll around Ashes Hollow or Batch Valley, or to enjoy the views from the top of the Ragleth, Lawley or Caradoc hills. Note the baskets of food for the picnic lying at their feet. The message to Miss Edwards of Cleobury Mortimer on the reverse of this postcard reads: 'We had a good day when this group was taken. Don't we all look sober. Hope you are all smiling. Love J & E'.

The pool in Cardingmill Valley, Church Stretton, was built to supply a good head of water to drive the water mill further down the valley. In the early part of the last century it was used by bathers who in the spring would have to share their swimming facility with thousands of tadpoles. Youngsters used to enjoy sailing their boats on the pool but quite often had to paddle out to retrieve them if the wind dropped. The pool was drained in the early 1960s and the site is now a car park, though you can still see the diving step and a notice stating the depth of three feet.

The entrance to Ashes Valley lies behind the Ragleth Inn at Little Stretton. The valley, with its picturesque slopes and winding track beside a gurgling brook, is ideal territory for ramblers and walkers. In April 1927 Barbara recounts her adventures on the back of this postcard to A.R. Edmondson, who lived in Cheshire: 'We have been quite a famous walk for the first day and even then it was all we could do not to be home for tea!! Went up Cardingmill Valley along the top and down Ashes Valley and over into Callow Hollow, which is awfully pretty. Then across the main road and railway - up the Ragleth and home as Pepys would say'.

The hounds of the South Shropshire Hunt are being exercised on land close to their kennels that are located up a narrow road just south of the village of Annscroft. At the beginning of the 20th century there were six packs of hounds kennelled within the borders of Shropshire. Before moving over to Annscroft the kennels of the hunt were at Plaish Hall near Cardington, which was the home of Mr J.C. Dun-Waters, the Master of Fox Hounds. The tiny shop stands isolated at a crossroads between Annscroft and Longden. The shop has shut and has been enlarged and converted into a private house. The photographer is looking back towards Shrewsbury with the road to the left taking you to Pontesbury. Note the advertising for Packer's Chocolate, Lyons Cakes and their coffee and chicory extract and Franklyn's Cutty First.

In the 1930s the countryside around Habberley was described as having 'an undulating surface, and presents many interesting views of picturesque beauty'. The lord of the manor and sole landowner in the area was Col. Frederick William Caton Jones, who lived at Earlsdale Pontesford. He was born in Australia and travelled around the world during his 32½ years of service in the British Army. In 1909 he won the Nagpur Hunt (Pigsticking) Cup. The church on the left is St Mary's Habberley and the house with the board over the door is the Mytton Arms Inn. The inn was small with only one parlour, a kitchen and back kitchen and four bedrooms. In 1901 the owner was Mr Heighway Jones of Earlsdale Pontesford and the landlord was James Jukes. The short note on the back of the postcard informs us that the young lady is H.M.N., with her dog Rip, in August 1931.

The Nelson Hounds assemble outside the Miners Arms in Minsterley for the stirrup cup before the hunt begins. The spectators are standing on the old bridge that was replaced in 1909. The hounds belonged to Mr William Nelson, the Master of the Hunt, who lived at Loton Park, Alberbury, but Mr David Davies MP, who lived at Llandinam in Montgomeryshire, hunted them. In 1900 the landlord of the Miners Arms was William Henry Ray, who advertised his hostelry as a hotel and brewery with good accommodation for commercial gentlemen and tourists. In 1901 Mrs Powell of Shadymoor in Dorrington owned the inn and the accommodation included two kitchens, a bar, a smoke room, a parlour, eight bedrooms and stables for 12 horses. By 1929 the Miners Arms Hotel was being run by the People's Refreshment House Association Ltd, which later changed its name to the Bridge Hotel.

The children and lady are fascinated by the photographer in Post Office Road, Minsterley. The village is fairly compact and has a variety of attractive houses. From an early date the post office was able to deal with letters, money orders and telegrams, and they had a savings bank and an annuity and insurance office. Letters for delivery arrived via Pontesbury at 6am and were despatched at 6.30pm. It is interesting to note that as late as 1922 the telephone service from the office was only available for places within a limited distance.

The huntsmen and hounds take a rest at a meet held in Little Stretton on 26 March 1914. Hunting was viewed differently at the beginning of the 20th century than it is today. Shropshire boasted that it was a famous hunting county, with six packs of hounds within its borders and others who came from outside to hunt at various times during the season. A report in 1902 states: 'The kennels of the South Shropshire Pack are at Plaish Hall, and they hunt the country south of the Severn. The kennels of the North Shropshire Pack are at Lee Bridge and the meets of this hunt are in a more level district, broken, however, by Pimhill, Grinshill and the Hawkestone Heights. The Wheatland Hunt as its name indicates, hunts over fertile country, between Bridgnorth and Much Wenlock, its headquarters being Cleobury North. The beautiful valley of the Teme affords sport for the Ludlow Hounds and the United Pack takes the wilder district around Bishop's Castle, having their respective kennels near the two towns. The Albrighton Kennels are at Whiston Cross, near Shifnal and the range is more than 35 miles in extent from Newport into Staffordshire. Well watered by pleasant, winding rivers and trout brooks, there is plenty of scope for hunting the otter and the Hawkestone Otter Hounds obtain fine sport in various parts of the county. Hares are fairly numerous, and the Tanat Side Harriers hunting that part of the county which lies around Oswestry and Llanymynech.'

The village of Longnor lies just off the busy A49 eight miles south of Shrewsbury. To enter the village before 1925 all vehicles had to cross the ford, while pedestrians could use the footbridge on the right. The name of Longnor stems from 'long alder', a type of tree that lines the banks of the Cound Brook, which runs through the village. At the beginning of the 20th century most of the villagers were farmers and farm labourers but there was a village shop, a blacksmith, a cobbler, a wheelwright and a miller. The watermill, which closed in the mid-1930s, can be seen in the centre of the view.

The Heather Brae Café stood in a lay-by to the right of the busy A49 just outside Leebotwood on the way to Church Stretton. The café looked over to the Lawley at the front and across the railway line to the Long Mynd at the rear. This bungalow-style restaurant was at its most popular during the 1950s and 1960s when hundreds of visitors from all over the Midlands would descend on the area for a weekend outing or a longer holiday in the beautiful south Shropshire countryside. The café was also well sited to pick up passing trade and people who stopped for petrol at the garage next door. It had a licensed restaurant, which provided a wide menu of three-course meals. Morning coffee and afternoon teas were catered for, and Dairy Belle, the 'Dainty Ice-cream', was available for the children. The restaurant and the garage have been demolished and in recent years a Little Chef was built close by, which has also closed.

These children are enjoying a nature ramble through the Dingle at Church Pulverbatch. Perhaps they are from the local elementary school in the village. They are with their teacher, who in 1905 was the wife of the headmaster Mr Charles Briscoe. At the beginning of the 20th century *Kelly's Directory* describes Church Pulverbatch as having 'much romantic scenery in the neighbourhood, and is in close proximity to Cothercutt Hill with the majestic Wrekin in the distance.'

This picturesque scene of rural life shows the Town Pool at Church Pulverbatch and is dated 20 July 1905. The message on the reverse to S. Rees Evans Esq. from E.B. reads: 'I thought this a pretty little postcard for your collection. You would remember seeing this pond at the top of the village just by Mrs Woodcock's. The ducks on the water belong to her.' There were two families called Woodcock in the village at this time and they were probably related. The head of the first family, Samuel Wall Woodcock, was a farmer, and the second, William Smith Woodcock, was a farmer and maltster and the owner of the Woodcock public house in Castle Pulverbatch, which was named after the family.

Being close to the Welsh border, it is not surprising that the remains of two other castles can be found in the Pulverbatch area. One was sited just north of Wilderley Hall, and was built to protect a road running north from the Long Mynd to the Severn Valley. The second, close to Church Pulverbatch, was later occupied by a farmhouse called Castle Place. It was sited in a natural depression and was sometimes known as Toppings Castle.

The Hope Valley runs through lovely wooded scenery from Plox Green to The Gravels. The area has been riddled with lead mines since Roman times and traces of the white spoil heaps can be seen on either side of the road. Edward Haycock designed the Church of the Holy Trinity in an Early English style. It was erected in 1843 and was made a parish church in 1860, formed from part of the parish of Worthen. The church lies to the side of the road in a beautifully landscaped graveyard, which is cut in two by a gurgling stream. The church is reached by crossing a narrow bridge and the whole setting is a haven of peace and tranquillity.

A heavy fall of snow in the 1930s turns Ludford into a beautiful Christmas card scene. The view is looking across the River Teme towards Ludford Bridge and the Charlton Arms. The tall chimneystacks of Cliff Villas are just to the left of the inn. E.L. Charlton, who was reputed to have fought the last duel in England, built the house in 1841. The house on the banks of the river was converted into a youth hostel in about 1949. Part of the building was once a tollhouse on the old road, but it was extended into a riverside home in the 19th century. Ludlow has had a youth hostel for many years; in the 1930s it was situated at 112 Corve Street.

This beautiful view of Bucknell was taken from Coxall Knoll, looking west towards Tueshill Wood. Peeping through the trees in the centre is St Mary's church, with the village scattered in a semi-circle around it. In the foreground is the railway line, with the station and signal box on the left. The arrival of the railway brought a great deal of prosperity to the village and local industries like tree felling thrived as the wood could be transported by rail to all parts of the country. The cutting of oak bark that was sent to Birmingham and Lancashire for tanning was also an important business and bark ricks like the one near the railway track could be seen all along the line.

This postcard was entitled 'Evening on the River Clun'. Whether it is close to the town of Clun or not is not stated and there is nothing in the photograph to give its precise location. However it is a pleasant scene of rural life in south Shropshire at the beginning of the 20th century, with two young boys watching three cows enjoy a last drink before they settle down for the night. One old Shropshire superstition believes that the lowing of cows is a well-known death token and if a cow lows in your face three times, it is a sure sign of death.

Not a car in sight on the main road out of Newcastle-on-Clun to Newtown across the border in Wales. The road follows the valley of the River Clun, travelling through Hall of the Forest, the location of a grey stone farm house, which has been identified as the house where Sir Robert Howard hid his lover Frances Villiers from her murderous in-laws for five years. The girl, aged just 15, had been tied to a bedpost and beaten every night until she agreed to marry Sir John Villiers, the brother of the Duke of Buckingham.

This large ivy-covered house with a mournful-looking cow and a duck pond at the front and an old weather boarded barn at the rear is Church House Farm in Clungunford. Between 1895 and 1909 Thomas Moseley a tenant farmer, occupied it, but after 1909 it was not listed in *Kelly's Directory of Shropshire* and may well have been incorporated into another farm. In 1900 the principal landowners in the area were John Rocke, described as lord of the manor, William Hurt-Sitwell of Ferney Hall, Clungunford, and Captain McNab of Preston in Lancashire.

AN OLD RHYME.

―――

" Clungunford, Clunbury, Clunton and Clun,
The four *drunkenest* places under the sun."
    Alas ! this was true of some far-away time,
    But now we have changed the original rhyme,
    We're ashamed of the character given long ago,
    Therefore *this* generation repeats the words so :—
" Clungunford, Clunbury, Clunton and Clun,
Are the *quietest* places under the sun."
    From " civilisation " we live a few miles,
    You may wander thro' meadows, and climb over stiles,
    Go up-hill or down, as it pleases your mind,
    And you'll meet only seldom with one of your kind.
    The hum of the insect, the song of the bird,
    The rustle of leaves by the soft breezes stirr'd,
    The lowing of cattle, the bleating of sheep,
    The running of water that lulls you to sleep,—
    These sounds you may hear, and more if you choose
    As you lie on the green-sward and lazily muse
    On the beauty around you, above and below,
    And watch, as you linger, the sunset's rich glow.

ANOTHER VERSION.

" Clunton and Clunbury, Clungunford and Clun
Are four *pretty* places under the sun."
    Motorist, cyclist, and artist declare
    The woods, hills and valleys are charmingly fair.
    The buildings are ancient, the ruins renown'd,
    And Camp, Dyke and Knoll with traditions abound.

A WISH.

" Clungunford, Clunbury, Clunton and Clun."
May they flourish as long as Clun River shall run.

                R.H.,
                Clun, Shropshire·

The first poem condemns Clungunford, Clunbury, Clunton and Clun as 'The four drunkenest places under the sun'. This could well be true. Situated in Clun at the end of the 19th century there were six public houses: the Castle, the White Horse, the Buffalo, the Six Bells, the Sun and the Crown. But to recommend the area to the tourist the poet goes on to recommend all its other amenities to motorists, cyclists and artists, declaring them the 'four prettiest places under the sun'.

This photograph of a man with three horses in a quiet country lane near Clun was entitled 'Out For The Night'. At the beginning of the 20th century horses still played a leading role in rural life and a good horse was always in demand and realised a good price. Jackson and McCartney held a horse sale at the South Shropshire and Central Wales Horse Repository in Craven Arms in June 1913. The entry of 180 horses was not as large as usual but this was due to farm work being behind schedule. Even so trading was reported as 'exceptionally keen'. There were buyers from London, Manchester, Liverpool, Birmingham, Wolverhampton, Bristol, Swansea and Bolton, and 35 of the best horses averaged 54 guineas each. The Championship Silver Cup for the best horse at the sale was won by E. Crowther, of the Llan farm in Clunton, for the best wagon gelding or mare, four years or over and suitable for town work.

Florrie Lock wrote this postcard on 22 July 1920 to her mother in London. She writes: 'Dear Mother, Its been pouring nearly all day, but I've managed to be out most of the time. I went with Di to Chelmick this afternoon and had tea there. The hedges were a mass of honeysuckle, wild roses, foxgloves etc. oh the scent was delicious. The heavy mists rather spoilt the views but still I quite enjoyed the walk in spite of the rain. In case I don't write again I expect to come home by the 1.20 from here, gets to Paddington 7.15. With love Florrie'. Old Star Lane in All Stretton is just off the main road and is named after a local family.

Chapter Eight
Castles, Halls and Houses

There have been almshouses at Ludlow for several centuries and they were closely associated with the parish church of St Giles. By the 16th century they had fallen into disrepair and were extensively renovated at the expense of William Foxe, who lived close by at Ludford House. The hospital was rebuilt around 1672 by Sir Job Charlton, who also endowed the charity with property and land. The Charltons had bought Ludford House from the Foxe family and Sir Job had a high-ranking job on the Council of the Marches. The almshouses were for 'six poor and impotent persons, one of whom was to be warden' and they were to be known as 'The warden and poor of the Hospital of Ludford'.

After visiting Ludlow in about 1587 Thomas Churchyard wrote in his book *Worthies of Wales* that Castle Lodge was 'The faire house of Mr Sackford's which he did build.' Early in the 16th century the lodge was used as a prison and was described as a hell by criminals sentenced by the Council of the Marches. In 1960 it was known as Castle Lodge Buttery, supervised by Donald Pearce. It had a high-class buffet service of good foods and a wide range of delicious drinks. Down Mill Street are the petrol pumps belonging to the Castle Garage, which was founded by J.D. Parsonage around 1930. Just beyond the garage is the Blue Boar Inn, reputed to be one of the first buildings in Ludlow to be built out of brick. When the inn first opened in the 17th century it was known as the Portcullis.

Ludlow Castle was built by the Normans on this natural defensive site overlooking the River Teme. Until 1689 it was the headquarters of the Council of the Marches, which maintained law and order along the border between England and Wales for several hundred years. After this date the castle was neglected and fell into ruin, but it soon became a focal point for artists, photographers, local historians and sightseers from all over the country. Compare the large open outer bailey to the cramped inner bailey, which is entered through the massive square keep. To the left of the keep are the Judges' Lodgings and in the centre of the inner bailey is the unique rounded Norman nave of St Mary Magdalene Chapel. Overlooking the River Teme are the living quarters, which include the Solar, Great Hall, Great Chamber, and Tudor lodgings. The Georgian panoramic walk can be seen circling the outside of the castle.

People travel from all over the world to visit Stokesay Castle, which is a wonderful example of a fortified manor. The settlement was originally called Stoke, but after the Norman Conquest in 1066, the land was given to the de Say family and was known as Stoke-de-Say, which was later abbreviated to Stokesay. Picot de Say was responsible for building the first castle on this site, but the building there today was erected in around 1280 by Laurence de Ludlow, a wealthy wool merchant. The oldest part of the building is the north tower on the left, which contains the well. The beautiful south tower can only be reached by a flight of steps from the outside of the building that leads to the private quarters of the Lord of the Manor. The Solar contains an unusual carved wooden fireplace and two peep holes that look down into the massive main hall.

The Grove was a Victorian mansion situated close to Craven Arms and the village of Wistanstow. John Jones, a prosperous ironmaster and banker, built it in 1878. His daughter Harriet married David Henry Green QC, the son of a former Governor of the Bank of England. They later occupied the mansion and Harriet continued to live there until World War Two when it was commandeered by the military. In 1949 the estate was sold and five years later the mansion was demolished. J.P. Wood and Sons, who had started trading in Craven Arms at the beginning of the 20th century, bought the estate in 1956. Over the next 40 years a thriving poultry business was developed, which at its height employed around 1,500 people and processed up to 500,000 chickens a week under the brand name 'Chukie Chickens'. In 1968 the business was sold to Unilever, who in turn sold it on to Unigate. The firm closed in the early 1990s. The lodge, which was erected in the early 20th century, is still standing.

Purslow Hall, which is situated near Clunbury, was described in *Kelly's Directory* for Shropshire in 1905 as 'An ancient, roomy, mansion of red brick, with two wings, and stands on an eminence, approached from the high road by a carriage drive through a plantation, with pleasure grounds in front sloping down to the river'. Parts of the house date back to the early 17th century but with later additions. It was once the home of Hugh Louis Heber-Percy, the son of Algernon Heber-Percy of Hodnet Hall. He was educated at Harrow and went cattle and sheep farming in Australia. He travelled extensively throughout the world, loved fishing and big game hunting and had a fine collection of trophies, heads and skins at Purslow that he had shot himself. Note the large black dog watching the photographer from the middle window of the left-hand bay.

Bedstone Court is a magnificent Elizabethan-style mansion, erected in 1884 by the architect Thomas Harris, the author of *Victorian Architecture*. It was built for Sir Henry Ripley MP, whose great-grandfather had made the family fortune by opening a dye works in Bradford. In 1900 Sir Henry was described as lord of the manor and sole landowner. The mansion, set in its own picturesque and ornamental grounds, is a 'Calendar House', having 365 windows, 52 rooms and 12 chimneys. The Ripleys later moved to Bedstone House, with the Court being taken over by the Langley family before being converted into a successful boarding school.

Hopton Castle dates from the 12th century and was named after the de Hopton family. In the 15th century it was passed by marriage to the Corbets, who sold it to the Wallop family. During the Civil War the castle was owned by Robert Wallop and was held by Parliamentary forces. In February 1644 the castle was attacked by a large Royalist army and although greatly outnumbered the defenders were able to withstand several attacks with a garrison of only 31 men. Only after inflicting huge casualties on the Royalist side, and after threat of being undermined, did the castle surrender. But instead of being imprisoned the 29 surviving Parliamentarians were brutally massacred, being forced to strip on a bitterly cold day and then being hacked to death with knives and swords. Two maids were also badly treated but managed to escape. This treachery is thought to have led to the saying 'a Hopton Quarter'. To prevent it being used again the castle was dismantled, leaving it in the state we see today.

Near the village of Lydbury North is the entrance to Walcot Park, which was once the home of the Earl and Countess of Powis. Lord Clive of India purchased the estate and the mansion was built for him in 1763. The architect was Sir William Chambers and the house once contained many treasures of the great man's life in the sub-continent. The Clive family left Walcot in 1933 to take up residence just across the border at Powis Castle in Welshpool. On the right of the gate is a bell tent, which was used by the local police, and at the far end of the drive is a uniformed man; perhaps the policeman is on duty.

Plowden Hall lies two and a half miles south-east of Bishop's Castle and has been the home of the Plowden family since Saxon times. The hall was built by Edmund Plowden on the site of an earlier house in about 1557. Inside much of the oak panelling and a fine Jacobean mantelpiece remains. There is also a family chapel with an unusual brass memorial representing Edmund's father Humphrey. The Plowdens were staunch Catholics and the house has a number of priest holes, from a large one descending from top to bottom along side one of the chimney stacks, to a smaller one beneath a bedroom floor, just large enough to accommodate a man standing.

This view across the lake to Clun Castle was taken in about 1930. Parts of the castle still remain but the lake has disappeared. The lake was man-made and lined with clay. After World War Two it was sold to a Birmingham businessman who, not knowing its history, tried to clean out the weed using a bulldozer; this disturbed the clay and the water leaked out. The lake used to power one of the water mills and was stocked with thousands of fish. The first castle was a motte and bailey construction, erected by Picot de Say, and it is mentioned in the Domesday Book. It was strategically placed and was in the first line of defence against attacks by the Welsh. The author Sir Walter Scott stayed for several months at the Buffalo Hotel in Clun, where he wrote his novel *The Betrothed*, basing his Garde Douleureux on Clun Castle. A large part of the keep still survives, as well as a section of curtain wall and two circular towers.

Clungunford Hall at Aston-on-Clun is the family seat of the Rocke family and was built between 1825 and 1828. One wing of the mansion housed 'the celebrated museum' of British birds and their eggs that were collected by John Rocke, who died on 3 April 1881. At that time the museum was described as 'one of the most perfect as to details and grouping to be met with', but today such collections are out of favour. Meredyth Evan Rocke was living in the Hall in 1937 and was listed as lord of the manor and chief landowner in the area. The family were very involved with the church, with Rockes being rectors of Clungunford in direct succession from the late 18th century until the middle of the 20th.

The occupants of Jordan's Cottages in Clunton are captured on this photograph taken at the beginning of the 20th century. All the men are at work, leaving two women, a boy, 10 girls, a kitten and a dog to enjoy the sunshine. There appears to be a person in bed but getting some fresh air through the open door on the left. The cottages are named after John Jordan, a wheelwright who lived there in the middle of the 19th century. There were a number of other tradesmen in the village at this time, including a mason, a miller, a shoemaker and a maltster. Note the lovely wicker pram by the hedge and the tin roof that has replaced the thatched one.

At the beginning of the 20th century the Cwm at Clunbury was the home of the Brettell-Vaughan family. Standing at the foot of the Black Hill in an estate of over 1,300 acres, it had a commanding view down the valley to Hopton Castle and across to the Clee Hills. Around 1900 the estate was known for its grouse and blackcock and for an excellent yearly crop of bilberries. Although the Earl of Powis is listed as lord of the manor in 1900, the Brettell-Vaughans are listed as one of the biggest landowners. Inside the church at Clunbury there are several stained-glass memorial windows dedicated to the family.

According to the old rhyme, 'Clunton, Clunbury, Clungunford and Clun are the quietest places under the sun'. This timber-framed and thatched cottage, known as Church House, Clunton, gives you a feeling of timelessness. William Hughes occupied the building in 1921. He was the Assistant Overseer of Clunbury but by 1929 he had moved and it was the home of Joseph Edwards, a farmer. As the 20th century progressed the village become even quieter with the closure of the Methodist Chapel, the school and the village inn. In recent years the trend has been reversed with the reopening of the Crown Inn. Just north-east of the village on top of Sunny Hill lies a magnificent Iron Age fort, proof of human activity in the area over hundreds of years.

Aston Hall in the village of Aston-on-Clun was one of four halls in Shropshire known by that name, the others being at Oswestry, Shifnal and Wem. This house, which was built in the 1820s, has five bays and a wonderful entrance porch supported by four Greek Doric columns. The hounds, horses and riders are just about to set off on a hunt after being fortified by a stirrup-cup. Note the servant with the tray of drinks by the hounds. The hall was occupied at this time by E.J. Artindale Esq., but by 1921 the Revd Sidney Dugdale, prebendary of Hereford Cathedral, was living there.

The Sylvester Horne Memorial Hall was opened on the High Street in Church Stretton in September 1918. It was erected by the Congregational Church in memory of Charles Sylvester Horne, a Congregational minister who had retired to Church Stretton. He died suddenly on 2 May 1914 while on a lecture tour of North America. His body was brought back to Church Stretton and he was buried in the town cemetery on 15 May 1914. The hall cost £3,000 and was built out of red brick with stone facings on the site of three almshouses and six cottages. The hall, which is now owned by the parish council, once had its own library and reading room. Sylvester Horne was the father of comedian Kenneth Horne, who is best remembered for his popular Sunday lunchtime radio programme 'Round the Horne'.

Tudor Cottage stands at the southern end of the High Street in Church Stretton. It is one of the oldest buildings in the town and was partly rebuilt after the great fire of 1593 that damaged a great deal of the town. At some point in its history the roof has been raised; the eaves of the old roofline can be seen in the northern wall on the left. The photograph was taken sometime in the 1940s as the sign on the lamppost directs the public to the nearest air-raid shelter.

The Malt House at Little Stretton was built in about 1500 and is a genuine box-framed building. At some point in its history the roof has been raised and a floor inserted above the open hall to give the building a second storey. An old cobbled floor remains in the cellar. Close by stood a large barn, unusually constructed out of vertical weather-boarding, but it has since been demolished. The Benbow family, who were maltsters and farmers, farming over 150 acres of land, occupied the house for many years.

Parts of the Manor House at All Stretton date from about 1600. For a time in the early 19th century it became a maltings, but was later used as a lodging house for tramps and was licensed to sleep 13 men, who had to spend the night standing up, with their arms over a rope strung across the room. They were woken in the morning by the landlord, who untied one end of the rope and let it drop. No food was supplied but any traveller who brought his own was allowed to cook it over the open fire. On the wall hung the following rules: 'No drinking allowed on the premises. No bad language to be used. No drums to be used here. No washing on Saturday or Sunday. No smoking upstairs. Couples to wash their own pots.' At the beginning of the 20th century the house was restored and was called the Manor House for the first time.

Marshbrook is a tiny village that lies three miles south-east of Church Stretton where a small stream rising on the Long Mynd meets the Quinny Brook to flow south to join the River Onny at the Grove near Craven Arms. Standing on a bank overlooking the main A49 is a timber-framed building known as the Old Post Office. It was built in the 16th century and has two small sandstone extensions.

Corfton Hall is a red-brick mansion, which was occupied in 1902 by Richard Alison Johnson. He was born in Devon in 1865 and was educated at Eton and Magdalene College, Cambridge. He was a keen huntsman and was the Master of the North Hereford Hounds between 1888 and 1893. He was a gentleman farmer who listed his other interests as salmon fishing, shooting and motoring, although he still kept his membership of the coaching club.

Many fans of the author Mary Webb travel to Pontesbury to see the house she was living in when she wrote the first of her great novels, *The Golden Arrow*, published in 1916. She was born Mary Gladys Meredith at Leighton Lodge in 1881. She married Harry Webb, a relative of Captain Matthew Webb, in 1912 and after two unhappy years in Weston-super-Mare they returned to Shropshire. They spent the next two years here in Pontesbury and as they were not very well off Mary used to sell produce she had grown in her garden at the market in Shrewsbury. They spent about two years in Pontesbury before moving to Spring Cottage on Lyth Hill. She suffered with illness for most of her life, dying at an early age in 1927. To commemorate her association with Pontesbury the local comprehensive school has been named after her.

This group of cottages situated just off the main road in Pontesbury were known as Birch Row. They dated from the 14th century, were cruck-framed and originally built as one dwelling. There was a central living area with an open hearth in the centre and a hole in the roof to let out the smoke. Such buildings are extremely rare but they were demolished in the 1950s to make way for a pair of modern houses. Several years before their demolition a galvanised roof replaced the lovely thatch. One of the last families to live there were the Corfields, who moved into 3 Birch Row in 1948 and were there until demolition.

Coal was extracted from the Shrewsbury Coalfield for many years from small mines scattered across the countryside to the south-west of the county town. Some of the pits installed steam engines, which were housed in tall narrow buildings. This is the coalfield's last surviving engine house, which is situated just off the main road at Pontesford. It is thought to have been built by Samuel or William Heighway in around 1800 and housed a beam-pumping engine. The engine had only a short life and had been removed by 1828. The building was converted into a dwelling by 1842. After many alterations, which include the rebuilding of the front face of the top storey in brick, the building has been turned into a very attractive property. The short message on the back of the postcard reads: 'This was one of Pollie's treasures'. Perhaps the lady on the front is Pollie with her family.

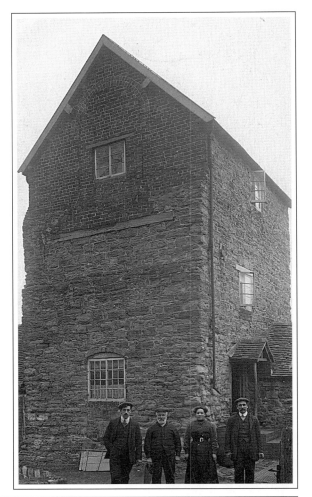

Plox Green stands on a cross roads about a mile south of Minsterley on the main road to Bishop's Castle. 'Plox' is probably derived from the name of the person who owned the land and the 'green' refers to a clearing in a forest. One of the turns off the main road takes you down a narrow lane to Ladyoak while the other takes you over a tributary of the Rea Brook and up to the mining village of Snailbeach and to the craggy peaks of the Stiperstones and Devil's Chair. In 1900 *Kelly's Directory* listed three farmers living in Plox Green, along with a blacksmith and wheelwright by the name of Jack Williams.

Sibdon Carwood is a small parish that lies one and a quarter miles west of Craven Arms. The castle is thought to be built on the site of a much older structure erected by the Corbet family in the 16th century. Parts of the present building date back to the middle of the 17th century but it was heavily restored in the 18th with the battlements being added in around 1800. The Corbet, Walcot and Fleming families owned the castle before it was occupied by the Holdens. During May 1907 auctioneers Morris, Marshall and Poole held a sale of the contents of the hall belonging to Fane Fleming Baxter in a large marquee. One of the highlights of the sale was the 'sharp tussle' between Mr Wright of London and Mr Williams of Stanway Manor Rushbury for 125 volumes of *The Gentleman's Magazine*. Mr Wright won the contest with a bid of £71. In the 1930s the owner was William Millington Holden, who was described as lord of the manor and principal landowner in the area. He was born in Nottinghamshire and served in the 6th Dragoon Guards and Royal Gloucestershire Hussars.

This is the impressive lodge that stands at the entrance to Netley Hall, a large estate situated about half a mile south of Dorrington. The hall is a three-storey building with a balustrade around the roof. It has five bays, a large porch resting on Tuscan columns and a clock turret over a side wing. It is built out of brick with a stone dressing from a design by Edward Haycock of Shrewsbury. It was built between 1854 and 1858 for the Hope-Edwards family, who were the sole owners of the land. The family always showed a great interest in the village of Dorrington and helped with the funding of the village church, school and hall.

This postcard is dated 24 April 1908 and the message to P. Headlam reads: 'Hanwood Mill, Residence of Mr and Mrs Blakeway Phillips and family. To be kept carefully. This is of great value'. There were two water mills in the village, this one and the Upper Mill. Both used the waters of the Rea Brook as a source of power, with this mill also using steam for grinding the corn. The Blakeway-Phillips family were running the mill in 1851 and continued to be the owners until about 1920, when the Cobden Flour Mills Co. Ltd bought it. The family had by this time moved to another house in the village called The Glen. The mill closed in 1925 and was bought by Thomas Kynaston of Hanwood House. It was converted into two houses, known as Mill House and Cobden House, in the early 1930s.

Thomas Corbett bought the Longnor Estate, but not the manorial rights, in 1610. The hall was started by Sir Richard Corbett in 1670 and completed by his son Uvedale in about 1694. It is a two-storey building with seven bays and is built out of red brick with a stone dressing. It has a hipped roof with a large central gable over the main entrance. The top of the gable was rebuilt in the 19th century and contains a circular feature depicting the Raven crest of the Corbett family. The family sold the hall in 1949 and for several years it was used as a country club.

Stanton Lacy lies three and a half miles north-west of Ludlow on the banks of the River Corve. Before 1066 it was a large village called Stanton. The suffix was added after the de Lacy family became the Norman lords of the manor. It is an attractive village with many different types of architecture, including some fine timber-framed houses. St Milburga, the daughter of King Penda of Mercia, founded the church of St Peter there. It was built close to the side of the river to commemorate the River Corve miraculously turning into a raging torrent to halt the progress of a Welsh Prince who had been pursuing her.

Six miles west of Clun and close to the Welsh border is the tiny hamlet of Bettws-Crwyn. The Welsh name means 'the Chapel of the Fleeces', which indicates the area's strong link with sheep farming. There is evidence that the settlement sits alongside a Bronze Age trading route that was later used by the cattle drovers from Wales into England. An unusual feature in the village church, which is dedicated to St Mary, is that the names of all the local farms are inscribed on the ends of the pews. In the early part of the 20th century, when this wintry scene was photographed, the Earl of Powis, lord of the manor, and William Garnett-Botfield of Decker Hill, Shifnal, were the principal landowners.

This is a rear view of Weir Cottage in Bucknell, which is a timber-framed cottage with a thatched roof. It is a single-storey building with a tall timber dormer window in the roof and a steep stone chimneystack at the gable end. Part of the right-hand side is also constructed out of weatherboard. The photograph was obviously taken in the spring as the Horse Chestnut tree to the left of the cottage is in flower. Note the chicken coop beneath the tree and the hayrick in the field.

This is Mr and Mrs Smith and their family at the rear of their home in Bucknell. Attached to their house was the largest of the village's grocery stores, known as Smith and Sons. After Mr Smith senior, the store was run by Frank Smith, who introduced the first van into the business, and then by Darry Smith and his wife Phyllis. The shop was sold as a going concern and remained open until around 2000, when it was turned into a private dwelling. From the left are: daughters Nell and Florry Smith, Bill Herbert, a cousin, and Mr and Mrs Smith.

The rector of a country church in the 19th century would expect to live a fairly easy and stylish life. The grand house in the centre with the walled garden and delightful pleasure grounds is the rectory at Clungunford. In 1851 the living was described as a 'Rectory, yearly value £538, with residence and 53 acres, two rods and 18 perches of glebe land, which was the gift of John Rocke the lord of the manor who lived at Clungunford Hall.' The rector at this date was the Revd Thomas Owen Rocke, a family member, who served there until 1882. The following year the Revd Frederick Cooke became curate-in-charge, a post he held until 1892, when the Revd William Charles Rocke was old enough to become rector, a post he held until the 1940s. In the middle distance is the Elementary School that was erected in 1855 to accommodate 158 children.

Hillside House stands on Longhills overlooking the entrance to Cardingmill Valley. It was built in the period at the end of the 19th century when the town was expanding and becoming a retirement centre. In the Shropshire section of his work on the *Buildings of England*, Nikolaus Pevsner writes: 'Half-timber is the hallmark of Church Stretton. The place became a resort between 1880 and 1900, and that was the time of the great fashion for neo-half-timbering, especially for gables, above brick storeys below. It is the popular form of new prettiness which came in with Norman Shaw and his pupils but is not always handled with Shaw's gusto'. Hillside, which was occupied for many years by two sisters called Hanan, is a good example of this type of architecture.

The Earl and Countess of Powis lived at Walcot Park for many years before moving to Powis Castle in Welshpool. One of the main features of the park is the serpentine lake to the north of the hall, which was constructed by French prisoners during the Napoleonic Wars. To maintain the day-to-day business of a large estate, agents were appointed to manage and to report back to the owners. In the early part of the 20th century R.H. Newill was the agent for the Earl of Powis at Walcot Park. Both the tenants and the workers on the estate held him in very high esteem. This was shown on the occasion of his silver wedding anniversary when Edward Hamar presented Mr and Mrs Newill with a silver candelabra with Corinthian pillars on behalf of the tenants and Henry Phillips presented them with a silver Queen Anne-style tea service on behalf of the workers. To celebrate, the Newills invited all the tenants and workers to a supper held in the schoolroom and catered for by Mr G. Edwards of the Powis Arms.

Hesterworth is situated half way between Hopesay and Aston-on-Clun, on the bank of a tributary of the River Clun. For a great deal of the 19th century the Beddoes family, who played a major role in the area for many years, occupied the house. In 1853 a school was erected at Hopesay through the generosity of a Miss Beddoes and there is a memorial window in the church in honour of Captain Henry Beddoes. Between 1879 and 1913 Mrs Beddoes was living at Hesterworth while Captain Thomas Henry Beddoes of the Royal Navy was listed as one of the principal landowners. Albert Watson and William Bland occupied the house for a short period until it was taken over by Major C.B. Habershon in 1926. The Habershon family were still there in July 1962 when they gave permission to the local Women's Institute to use the grounds of Hesterworth for a garden fête. The fête had many attractions, which included a fortune teller, a baby show and a guess the weight of a sheep competition. During the evening a dance was held and the whole event made a grand total of £322 8s 3d.

Chapter Nine
Fêtes, Fun and Festivities

In the early years of the 20th century the boys of Ludlow Grammar School would put on an entertainment in the Town Hall. The shows were given to raise money to promote school activities, the cause in 1906 being the sports club. There was a large attendance and an excellent programme was presented, which included the Revd T. Hawkes singing *The Postillion*, a display on the parallel bars, and a play entitled *The Monks' Stratagem*. The main figures in the play were Leonard (the missing heir) played by H.S. Harris, Sir Pounds de Weight by H.K. Paffard, Lady Pounds by P. Lander, Abbot Tumbo by A.T. Diggle, Linda (Sir Pounds' daughter) by T.F. Sankey and Jack Daw (the jester) by P.V. Perry. Written on the reverse of this postcard, which was sent by George to Miss F. Reason in Cambridge, was the following message. 'I am sending you a postcard of our play last night. They done it very well indeed. We got a good bit of money this time. We did not have to go to school this morning til 9.30.'

Early in November 1909 rumours spread around Ludlow of an imminent royal visit as the Prince and Princess of Wales were to be guests of the Earl of Powis at Welshpool and were expected to visit the Earl of Plymouth at his home at Oakley Park, Bromfield, following a short tour of Ludlow. Unfortunately the Princess arrived on her own but the citizens of Ludlow gave her an enthusiastic welcome on a gloriously fine day. She was officially welcomed by the Mayor of Ludlow, Councillor G. Woodhouse, at the Corve Bridge. He then escorted her through the town to the Castle and St Laurence's Church, where she made a lengthy stop at each. The Princess is seen walking down Castle Street towards Broad Street. She wore a mole-coloured costume with blue fox furs and a feathered toque. Before leaving for Oakley Park and lunch with the Earl of Plymouth the Princess shook hands with the Mayor, expressing her thanks for all the interesting sights she had seen.

B.G. Huck, who was touring the country with his Bleriot monoplane, arrived in Ludlow in 1913. He was greeted by the Mayor of Ludlow Mr E.T. Evans JP. Known as 'Flying' Huck, he flew his plane from Ludford Park and gave rides to those wealthy enough to afford the 10-shilling fee. Huge crowds were attracted to the grounds, curious to see an aeroplane for the first time. During his visit to Shropshire he also performed in Shrewsbury and Market Drayton. Flying was still in its infancy at this time and extremely dangerous. In August 1913 the famous aviator Col. Cody was killed with his engineer Evans at Fleet in Hampshire. Mr Huck also died prematurely, but not from a flying accident; he died from an attack of pneumonia in 1916.

A great crowd of people gather in Lower Broad Street to see the aftermath of a fire that destroyed a great deal of Bodenham & Sons Ltd warehouse on 28 July 1908. Captain Parker and his fire crew fought the blaze but were unable to contain it and within the hour the roof had collapsed and the building was gutted. Part of the building was occupied by J.W. Price, a wicker furniture manufacturer who lost more than £600 of stock, which he had fortunately insured. It was thought the fire was caused by a furnace in the south end of the building overheating. The warehouse had been erected in the 19th century by William Evans, a cloth manufacturer. During its short history the building had been affected by several fires and after the last, in the second half of the 20th century, it was demolished. Note the fireman on the ladder damping down and the pile of furniture on the pavement outside.

This interesting event, 'The Christening of the Boats', took place on the River Teme at the bottom of Mill Street in Ludlow in 1904. It was organised by the Ludlow Attractions Committee and three boats were christened the *Whitcliffe*, the *Ludlow Castle* and the *Harry Lloyd*. They christened another boat the *Alice* the following year and in 1907 the Mayoress Mrs Bodenham christened four more boats. They were the *King Edward*, the *Windsor*, the *Comus* and the *Arts and Crafts*. In 1913 another christening was carried out by another Mayoress, Mrs Evans, when two more boats, the *King George* and the *Princess of Wales*, were added to the fleet. At this event it was stated that the Attractions Committee now had an excellent stretch of river and 10 good boats to hire out. It was also reported that in the whole time they had been hiring out boats they had never had an accident and no one had drowned. After the ceremony the Mayor and Mayoress, accompanied by their daughter, were taken for a row on the river in *King George*.

This photograph showing Ludlow's Boy Scouts parading on the Castle Green was probably taken during a visit by the movement's founder Lord Baden-Powell in 1910. The Scouts were founded in 1907 and proved very popular with many youngsters transferring from the Boys' Brigade, which caused a certain amount of friction between the two groups. At the outbreak of World War One they were given a number of important jobs, including one for the Chief Constable of Shropshire, who asked them to protect all the telephone and telegraph lines between Chester and Hereford. Without delay troops of Scouts were summoned from all over the county to carry out 24-hour guard over 50 miles of wire. They were provided with a notebook and pen and told to report suspicious characters to the police.

This small house fire occurred at 13 Broad Street in the 1920s. The premises was then occupied by Miss Sarah Frances Smith and was known as the Fancy Warehouse, selling a variety of goods that would have included wool and other items of haberdashery. The photograph was taken by Walter Harper, a local photographer, whose studio was ideally situated on the opposite side of the road. The lorry just below the building belonged to John Bowdler, a builder from Brand Lane.

Mr Hugh Heber-Percy JP is replying to the vote of thanks at a garden party and bazaar held in the grounds of Purslow Hall on 1 August 1907. The event was held to raise money for the Clunbury Nursing Club, which was formed in 1902. A marquee was erected on the lawn, which was filled with stalls and an area to serve afternoon teas. There was a dairy stall laden with dressed poultry and dairy produce and a stall full of fireproof ware and white china services. A fine gallery of watercolours depicting local beauty spots and painted by C. Gilchrist Clarke were on display, priced at 30 shillings each. Other stalls were selling books, embroidery, art pottery, Italian inlaid woodwork, clothing, fancy articles and attractive bric-à-brac. Outside under the trees, dancing mice and a well-bred retriever puppy were offered for sale and there was a twopenny bran tub for the children. Other attractions included the Shrewsbury Society of Pierrots who sang in 'duets and trios' and performed 'screaming sketches' in a half-hour concert. To add a touch of class to the proceedings, Mrs Roses' String Orchestra from Ludlow played at intervals throughout the afternoon. Note the beautiful gramophone with the large horn on the right and just to the side of the table the black dog that was seen in the window of the Hall.

The Bucknell Show ran for about 12 years during the 1920s and 1930s and was always held on the second Friday in August. Virtually the whole village took part and the day was full of fun and merrymaking. One of the entrants was this donkey cart and its four occupants. It is parked outside the village post office. The cart belonged to Arthur Whittle, the man on the left. He was the local postman but in his spare time he used his donkey and cart to carry coal and other goods from the railway station and around the village. The man on the right holding the fiddle is Stan Whittle.

These gentlemen belong to Bishop's Castle Amateur Minstrel Troupe, which was very much in demand and used to entertain at various functions in and around the town. The two men standing on either side of the troupe have been identified. The one on the left is William Heaven, a hairdresser from Church Street, while the one on the right is Albert Bright, whose party piece was the popular song *Boiled Beef and Carrots.*

The Bishop's Castle Town Band lead the parade back up the High Street after a service at the church to celebrate Hospital Sunday. It was an event that would have been repeated around Shropshire on a Sunday in July to raise money to support the work of the Royal Salop Infirmary, the county's leading hospital. The band would have been playing all the way down to the church, but on the way back they are saving breath to tackle the one-in-three gradient back to the Market Square. The banner reads 'Help Bishop's Castle to support the Royal Salop Infirmary'. The banner also tells us that the photograph was taken after 1914, as the title 'Royal' was not conferred on the hospital until July that year, when King George V visited Shrewsbury to attend the Royal Agricultural Show being held on the Racecourse at Monkmoor.

Although Bishop's Castle is many miles away from London, the death of Edward VII had a profound effect on the people of the town. The Borough Standard was flown at half-mast, as were the Union Flags over the Castle Hotel and the parish church. The wearing of mourning emblems was observed in the streets and the homes and shops in the town partially drew their blinds until after the funeral. A message of loyal sympathy was sent to the royal family by the town council via the Home Secretary. It read: 'The Mayor, Aldermen and Burgesses of Bishop's Castle in council assembled, beg humbly to offer to his Majesty the King, Queen Alexandra and the Royal Family their loyal sympathy with them in their sorrow and loss, they together with the Empire have sustained by the death of their most beloved and lamented King Edward'. It was signed by the Mayor, Councillor Adam Scott. On 10 May 1910 Town Clerk Mr Ernest Griffith reads out the Proclamation of King George V to the loyal subjects of Bishop's Castle. The Town Band and a large crowd gathered in the Market Square to witness the scene and, led by the men on the left waving their hats, gave three rousing cheers for their new monarch before singing the National Anthem.

The Bishop's Castle Bazaar and Fête was held over three days at the end of August in 1907. The fête was held in the vicarage grounds to raise funds for a new organ for the church. On the first day the fête was opened at three o'clock by the Countess of Powis and the following day by Mrs George, the Mayoress. The music was provided by the Town Band and there was dancing each evening between eight and 10 o'clock. Attractions over the three days included a pastoral play, concerts, air rifle practice, hat trimming and making competitions, an antique stall and amusements. There were also flower and fruit stalls and a refreshment and tea tent and on the last day a jumble sale. Admission on the first day was 1 shilling before six o'clock and 6d after, with prices on the second and third day set at 6d and 3d. Cheap rail fares to the fête were also available from Craven Arms and the intermediate stations. The Countess of Powis is the lady in the light dress in the centre. She was accompanied around the ground by her mother (on the right) and the Revd C.E. Warner, vicar of Bishop's Castle from 1898 to 1920. The event was hailed a great success and raised a total of £243.

The flags are flying brightly and the Bishop's Castle Town Band is accompanying the schoolchildren singing patriotic songs for the Empire Day celebrations in 1913. They are standing outside the Town Hall at the top of the High Street. The message on the back of the postcard asks Miss Aitken in Chorley if she can see Viv and Jessica with their Daddy, possibly standing just to the right of the Hall. Although the day was supposed to be fun it was reported that as the anniversary fell on a Saturday the schoolchildren were disappointed: the day was usually observed as a holiday and they had been deprived of it.

The celebrations for the Coronation of King George V in Bishop's Castle on 22 June 1911 began in the Market Square where a large crowd gathered. A new Borough Standard, a Coronation gift from Mrs Garnett-Botfield, was hoisted for the first time over the Town Hall and a parade was formed and led through the town to a Civic Service in the Methodist Church. The parade included the Mayor, Dr Selwyn Puckle, Town Clerk Ernest Griffith, civic dignitaries, Boy Scouts, orders from the Oddfellows and Foresters and local citizens. They marched through the town, which was described as 'a blaze of colour embellished with bright hued bunting, greenery, summer blooms and streets spanned with streamers'. They returned to the Square where the children from the infants' school, all smartly dressed and waving flags, joined them. The Coronation Hymn and the National Anthem were sung before each child in the town was presented with a Coronation mug. The Mayor, selected guests and the Town Band, led by J. Lewis, then attended a special dinner before the start of the afternoon events. The shop on the left belonged to H. and J. Edwards, who were listed as grocers, drapers and agents for W. & A. Gilby Ltd, wine and spirit merchants.

The Coronation celebrations resumed at the Bowling Green Close at three o'clock with a full programme of athletics. Prizes of 5 shillings, 2s 6d and 1 shilling were given to the first three competitors in each event. The winners and the runners up in the tug of war were given 12 shillings and 8 shillings, while the finalists in the pillow fight competition were each given 7s 6d. A sumptuous tea was served between 3.30 and 5.30pm for over 1,000 people in a large marquee. This was followed by dancing between seven o'clock and nine o'clock, which was accompanied by the Town Band. The people of Bishop's Castle love to dress up in fancy costumes and parade though the streets of the town and many hours were spent preparing their costumes for the big day. Note the patriotic John Bull and his dog at the front of the group and the real police constable on the left. At nine o'clock they led a torchlight procession through the town to Colebatch Hill, where a bonfire was lit as a finale to this enjoyable but historic event. Throughout the day Mr Roberts at the Three Tuns Brewery had fired the Royal Salute and the inmates at the workhouse were treated to a fine dinner.

This unknown event could be the parade forming for the annual Hospital Sunday that was held every July. The Mayor is Dr Selwyn Puckle and he is standing in the shop doorway of John Cooke and Son, the shoemakers. Ernest Griffith, the Town Clerk, stands just to the right in his wig and two mace bearers prepare to escort the Mayor. The men wearing the sashes are from the Order of Oddfellows. The ladies in their fine hats are standing outside Annie Hughes' stationery and printing shop and the poster to the left is advertising the Bishop's Castle Show on Tuesday 7 August.

The Bishop's Castle Band pose proudly for this photograph taken on 22 June 1911, the day of King George V's Coronation. The band was always very much in demand for parades, sports days, fêtes and dances and at an event like the Coronation they would have been playing for most of the day. The band also used to accompany the singing of hymns in church and once a week would serenade the Mayor outside his house.

The Countess of Powis opened Lydbury North Sale of Work, which was held in aid of the Church Organ Fund, on 3 September 1913. The Countess, who had travelled over from Welshpool, is posing with the Revd Bernard Keble Kissack MA, vicar of Lydbury North from 1912 to 1919. He later became the Hon. Chaplain to the Bishop of Ripon, rural dean of Knaresborough and canon of Ripon before retiring to Monmouth in 1955. The Countess was formerly the Hon. Violet, younger daughter and co-heir of the 12th Baron Conyer. She married the Earl of Powis in 1890. After introducing the Countess the vicar spoke of the need for a good organ in the parish church and hoped that the sale 'would prove eminently satisfactory'. The churchwardens, Mr R.H. Newill and Mr W.H.B. Whitaker, probably the gentlemen to the left of the vicar, also heartily thanked the Countess for her attendance.

Lydbury North Sale of Work was held in the garden belonging to Mr Newill, the agent for the Walcot Park Estate. The sale commenced at three o'clock and continued until dusk. The ladies of the parish ran five stalls and there was a rummage sale for the poorer villagers that started at five o'clock. The stall on the left is full of fancy goods and embroidery, while the stall to the right appears to have a variety of china and pottery laid out for the visitors to inspect. From their dress the visitors seem to be members of the middle and upper classes and quite often entrance charges to these social gatherings were set high at the beginning of a fête to deter the working classes. Newspaper reports often reveal that a fête or bazaar was 'attended by a large and fashionable gathering'. Business at the stalls and at the rummage sale was reported as brisk and the afternoon raised over £62. Note the baby in the centre who is still dressed in 'long clothes'.

Henry Howard, the Earl of Northampton, founded Holy Trinity Hospital in Clun in 1614. It was built to house 12 poor men who were to live a life of piety and to pray each day for the soul of their benefactor. In return the almsmen received 10 shillings a week, three tons of coal a year, a faggot of wood a month, clothing, a pint of milk and a pint of beer a day and a free dinner on Sundays and feast days, which were eaten in the hall. During the meal an old rule stated that, 'The Said Warden and Poor Men shall not at the time of their meals, nor at any other time, use any idle, scurril, scoffing, jesting or unbeseemingly talk or behaviour, but shall in all things quietly, soberly, civilly and modestly demean themselves'. Standing outside the hospital are 14 almsmen with the Revd Harold Scott, their resident chaplain from 1900 to 1927.

Standing outside his home in the quadrangle of Holy Trinity Hospital Clun is almsman Billy Cantie. The photograph, taken in about 1910, shows him in the blue cloak and top hat worn by all almsmen for church on Sundays; the large red and silver badge shows the arms of their founder, the Earl of Northampton. On Sundays it was expected that 'The Warden and all the Poor Men that are able to travel so far, shall every Sunday and Holiday resort orderly, by two and two together, in their livery gowns, to the parish church of Clun, to hear morning and evening prayers and sit in the seats belonging to the hospital, in seniority as the Warden shall appoint, where they shall reverently and devoutly behave themselves and then return again together by two and two to the hospital'. Billy came to the Hospital from Clunton where his brother Jack was a butcher.

The Madeley Prize Band leads the procession through the streets of Clun to celebrate the Coronation of King George V and Queen Mary on 22 June 1911. Following the band are able-bodied almsmen in their Sunday outfits and the schoolchildren all in their Sunday best. The *Ludlow Advertiser* reported, 'Never previously did the ancient town look gayer or more picturesque. Resident and business establishments were profusely decorated with Royal Colours, greenery, emblems and summer blooms and bright-hued streamers adorned the streets.' The day was organised by the Revd Machen, Mr Morgan George and Mr R. Haynes, who were congratulated for their efforts. The parade is passing George Mead's seed warehouse on the left. Mr Mead was listed as a grocer, ironmonger, oil and seed merchant and cycle and accessory agent, whose store was in the Market Place.

The children of Clun march up Church Street with their flags and garlands at the start of the Coronation Day celebrations. The parade was formed in the Square and led through the town by the Madeley Prize Band to the Parish Church, where the authorised Coronation Service was taken by the rector, the Revd Machen, and his curate, while the singing of patriotic hymns was led by the church choir.

At half-past one after the service in St George's Church, Clun, each child in the town assembled in the school yard and was presented with a Coronation mug by Mrs Machen, the rector's wife, and Mrs Haynes, the wife of Richard Haynes, a local printer from Ford Street. Note the lady on the right in her wonderful floral outfit and lace hat with flowers and veil. Sports were held in the Old Castle Grounds during the afternoon. The quarter-mile race was won by T. Gwilt, the schoolgirl skipping race by E. Pugh and the girls 100 yards by M. Jones. T. Price won the same event for the boys while W. Gittins won the unusual Bun and Treacle race for boys. G. Sherry won a special quarter-mile race for married farm workmen.

Between 2pm and 4.30pm a 'bountiful tea' was served by Mrs Arthur Morris, the wife of the local baker in Clun. Over a thousand guests attended and the schoolchildren, seated at their school desks, were able to use their new Coronation mugs for the first time. Other events during the day included a six-a-side football match, a tug-of-war competition won by a team from Bicton and a sheep chase. The chase offered a great deal of 'hilarity as the animal raced away in great style towards Bicton' followed by a horde of excited youths and young men. During the evening the villagers danced to the music of the Madeley Prize Band. The parishioners of Chapel Lawn and Bryn who had been invited to participate also enjoyed the festivities at Clun.

A group of little girls with brightly coloured parasols bring up the rear of Clun Show parade. Around 1900 the show became an annual event and is still held every year in August. The show is a success because the people of Clun and the surrounding villages enjoy dressing up and taking part in all the events. The parade always started at the church and would make its way down the steep gradient of Church Street and over the bridge. From there it wound its way up Bridge Street to the High Street and through the Square where it turned right into Enfield Street and on to the Castle Grounds, where all the main events were staged. Note the lady in the floral dress ushering the children over the bridge and just above her a man wearing a facemask rattles a box as he tries to entice a donation from the ladies sitting on the bridge. Just to the right of the bridge is the workshop and yard of John Roberts, the monumental mason.

People would gather on the steep slope in the Castle Grounds to watch the variety of events taking place in the arena throughout the day. They consisted of horse leaping and pony races, athletics, children's races and tug-of-war. This last event was very popular and taken very seriously by teams of young labourers from the surrounding area. Novelty events also took place, like this football match in the 1920s using a large ball advertising the *Daily Mail*. There was also a special race for the ladies, which included washing clothes in a tub and running with them to a washing line to hang them out.

One of the great attractions of the Clun Show was the Maypole Dray, which carried the 15 maypole dancers around the town to the Castle Grounds. In the early years the dray was decorated the night before with wild flowers, but in later years it was the young girls who wore the flowers in a garland around their hair. The dray and horse's harness was also plaited with flowers. The girls wore white cotton dresses that were tied at the waist with coloured satin ribbons. This photograph was taken at the 1908 show.

The maypole dancers pose for this photograph at the 1908 Clun Show. When the dray carrying them around the town arrived at the Castle Ground the maypole was set up on a flat surface near the river and the girls would dance at intervals throughout the day. The second girl to the right of the maypole is Ruth Evans, who lived at 11 Castle Street in Clun. She sent this postcard to her friend, Miss Dallas Smith of 20 Chester Mews, Regent's Park, London, informing her that she was the dancer marked with a cross. The girls practised hard for several weeks before the show and one of their favourite dances was known as 'In and out of the windows'.

The vicar of Clun, the Revd Alfred Kenyon, is standing to the right of the table contemplating the weather, as the ladies of Clun try to set out the cake table under the shelter of a tree in the grounds of the vicarage garden. The Sale of Work and Garden Fête was held on 21 June 1907 and was organised by the lady members of the congregation. Mrs Heber-Percy of Purslow Hall gave 'a fitting little speech' to open the event and through the kindness of the vicar a room was opened up in the vicarage for serving teas. The local paper commented that although the fête was held in 'inclement weather', it was a great success, raising over £26 for the annual outing of the parish choir.

This view is taken from the bridge in Clun during the flood of November 1907 that was brought on by melting snow and heavy rain up the valley, which is always a dangerous combination. To the right is Bridge Street and opposite where the boys are standing is Buffalo Lane leading up to the Square. The building on the right is the home of William Whitefoot, who ran a small grocery shop at the rear of his house in Buffalo Lane. By 1905, to supplement his income, he had taken on the responsibilities of income tax collector and sanitary inspector to Clun Rural District Council. During a bad flood the floodwater often entered his house through the front room window. Bob Davies occupied the house on the other side of Buffalo Lane for many years.

The Ancient Order of Foresters line up with the band outside the Kangaroo public house at Aston-on-Clun in 1907. The village had its own lodge of Foresters and there were other lodges in Clun, Craven Arms and Lydbury North. They were often involved in the organisation of local events, as well as parading around the villages several times a year, calling on local dignitaries and at hostelries for food and refreshment. They also encouraged young lads to enrol from a very early age. The Kangaroo is reputed to be the only inn of that name in the country. The owner of the inn was Edward Marston of Ludlow and the managers were Richard and Louisa Penny. In 1901 the accommodation at the inn was considered good but the building did need repairing. Most of their trade came from men working on the land and also passing travellers.

Not many postcards were printed of Stanton Long and this is a very rare view of village life at the beginning of the 20th century. The village lies off the main Craven Arms to Much Wenlock road, about a mile south-east of Shipton. Although never a large settlement, the village is situated in the fertile countryside of the Corvedale and agriculture has always been the main source of work in the area – the Harvest Home festival would have been an important event in the farming year. In 1900 the population of the village was made up of farming stock, a wheelwright and a carpenter; but there was no post office, village shop, school or public house.

A young man and his dog show great interest in the motorist attempting to negotiate the flood waters of the River Corve on the Bromfield road. Judging from the dark sky and the umbrella on the left the rain is still falling heavily. After a prolonged period of heavy rain the water quickly runs off the hillsides down the many small tributaries of the Corve, causing severe flooding. This is probably the summer flood of June 1924. Note the trees in the background have all their leaves.

Friendly Societies were very popular in south Shropshire at the beginning of the 20th century. There were Oddfellows Lodges at Clunbury and Bishop's Castle and Ancient Order of Foresters Lodges at Aston-on-Clun, Craven Arms and Lydbury North. As well as looking after sick members and those who had fallen on hard times, the lodges were often involved in the organisation of local events. They would also parade around the villages several times a year, calling on local dignitaries for food and refreshment. They dressed in their Sunday best and wore collars, sashes and bowler hats. They also carried large, beautiful, silk embroidered banners to signify which lodge they belonged to. The Oddfellows met at Norbury on Wednesday 6 July 1910. They were led by the Bishop's Castle Town Band around the villages, in poor weather, to the church in Norbury. After the service the Festive Board was held in a large marquee and was presided over by the Mayor of Bishop's Castle, Councillor A. Scott. During the speeches it was announced that £119 7s 10d had been spent on sick pay to members and £216 4s 8d in other payments. These men are Foresters leaving Hopesay Church. Note the younger members on the left and the banner depicting the Good Samaritan and the legend, 'Go Thou And Do Likewise'.

Bibliography

Bilbey, D., *A History of Church Stretton*, Phillimore & Co., 1985.

Hobbs, T., *The Pubs of Ludlow*, Logaston Press, 2002.

Kelly's Directory of Shropshire, various dates.

Leonard, J., *Churches of Shropshire and Their Treasures*, Logaston Press, 2004.

Lloyd, D., *A Concise History of Ludlow*, Merlin Unwin, 1999.

Lloyd, D., *Ludlow*, Chalford, 1995.

Lloyd, D. & G. Thomas, *Ludlow: A Second Selection*, Chalford, 2000.

Meech, J., *Shropshire Towns and Villages*, Sigma Leisure, 2000.

Mercer, E., *English Architecture to 1900: The Shropshire Experience*, Logaston Press, 2003.

Moore, R.K., *Memories of Clun*, Shropshire Libraries, 1986.

Moran, M., *Vernacular Buildings of Shropshire*, Logaston Press, 2003.

Pentabus, *Bucknell in View*, c.1985.

Pevsner, N., *Shropshire*, Penguin Books, 5th Edition, 1989.

Preshous, J., *Bishop's Castle Well Remembered*, 2nd Edition, 1995.

Raven, M., *The Shropshire Gazetteer*, M. Raven, 1989.

Shropshire W.I., *The Shropshire Village Book*, Countryside Books, 1988.

Shropshire W.I., *Shropshire Within Living Memory*, 1992.

Speight, M., *Ludlow in Old Postcards*, Zaltbommel/Netherlands, 1983.

The Victoria History of Shropshire Vols 1–4, 8 and 10.